Youth Spirit 2

PROGRAM IDEAS FOR CHURCH GROUPS

Collected from over 15 years of the phenomenal Christian education curriculum and worship resource *The Whole People of God*, these volumes offer tried and true material in easy-to-use format. These are proven resources with a theology and approach that thousands have come to trust.

Youth Spirit 2

PROGRAM IDEAS FOR YOUTH GROUPS

WOOD LAKE BOOKS INC.

Editor: Mike Schwartzentruber

Cover design: Margaret Kyle

Cover photograph: Duncan Harte, Lois Huey-Heck

Illustrations: Barbara Houston, © copyright Wood Lake Books Inc.

Permission to quote

The Gospel According to the Simpsons. © 2001 Mark I. Pinsky.
Used by permssion of Westminster John Knox Press.

Get 'Em Talking by Youth Specialties Inc. Copyright © 1989 by
Youth Specialties Inc. Used by permission of Zondervan.

From Gender Stereotypes to Equality. Used by permission of the
Division of Mission, the United Church of Canada.

Personal Pilgrimage, copyright © 2000 Viki Hurst; and *Celtic
Parables* © 1998 Robert Van de Weyer, used by permission of
Northstone Publishing.

"Prepare," by Ralph Middlecamp. Used by permission of *Ministry
and Liturgy Magazine,* 160 E. Virginia St., San Jose, CA 95112.

"Reaching Out in Toronto," by June Callwood, in *Maclean's,*
September 15, 1997. Used by permission.

"How to Watch Your Brother Die," by Michael Lassell. Used by
permission of the author.

"In the Beginning," from Top Gear, Joint Board of Christian
Education, Melbourne, 1993. Used by permission of Uniting
Education, P. O. Box 1245, Collingwood 3066, Australia.

"Bahá'i Prayer" by Bahá 'ulláh, from *Bahá'i Prayers* © 1982, 1985.
Used by permission of the National Spiritual Assembly of the
United States and the Bahá'i Publishing Trust of the United
States.

"Opening Up," by Roddy Hamilton. Used by permission of the
author.

"The REAL Monopoly Story," condensed from an article by Alyson
Huntly; from *World Wind Magazine for Children*, Vol. 17, No. 1,
1995. Division of Communication, The United Church of
Canada. Used by permission.

Canadian Cataloguing in Publication Data

Perry, Cheryl, 1970 –
 Youth spirit 2
 Includes index.
 ISBN 1-55145-500-5
1. Church group work with youth. 2. Christian education –
Activity programs. I. Title.
BV4447.P47 2002   259'.23   C2001-911641-1

Printing 10 9 8 7 6 5 4 3 2 1

Published by

Wood Lake Books Inc.

9025 Jim Bailey Rd

Kelowna, BC V4V 1R2

www.joinhands.com

Printed in Canada by
Transcontinental Printing

Wood Lake Books Inc. acknowledges the financial support of
the Government of Canada, through the Book Publishing
Industry Development Program (BPIDP) for our publishing
activities.

At Wood Lake Books we practice what we publish, guided
by a concern for fairness, justice, and equal opportunity in all
of our relationships with employees and customers.

We recycle and reuse and encourage readers to do the
same. Resources are printed on recycled paper and more
environmentally friendly groundwood papers (newsprint),
whenever possible. The trees used are replaced through
donations to the Scoutrees for Canada program. A percentage
of all profit is donated to charitable organizations.

Table of Contents

(DISCIPLES)

Contributors

....

We wish to thank the following people for their contributions to the book.

Julie Elliot
Adele Halliday
Clare Haman
Roddy Hamilton
Barbara Hampton
Duncan Harte
Brad Lavenne
Heather Malnick
Donna Scorer

How to Use this Book

Youth leaders are always looking for great ideas for weekly gatherings. But unlike Sunday morning programs, there is no "curriculum" to follow. So youth leaders spend a lot of time planning – gathering ideas from books of cooperative games, ice breakers, outreach projects, drama, devotions, crafts – to create programs. This book provides a wealth of great ideas for youth groups and their leaders. Some of the material has been adapted from Youth Paks of *The Whole People of God* congregational resource. Some of it has come from the shared experiences of people working weekly with real-life youth groups.

Instead of providing outlines for "canned" programs, the material in this book is organized according to themes on Idea Pages. These pages encourage leaders to pick and choose activities, building their own unique programs. (We suggest a method for doing this in the Introduction.)

Each Idea Page offers a variety of suggestions. These include games, crafts, discussion starters, reflection questions, and project ideas, as well as a group check-in and a closing worship. Idea Pages also suggest additional print resources and helpful websites.

Idea Pages are grouped into sections according to the seasons of the Christian Year. Each section begins with a description of the church season – its mood and flavor, special days, and implications for youth ministry. Many denominations organize their worship and church life following the Christian Year and the lectionary. With this book organized in the same way, we hope you will easily find activities to involve your group in the life and work of the larger church community. The book begins with the Season after Pentecost. This coincides with early autumn in North America, when school reconvenes after summer holidays and most youth programs are starting up.

Stories, graphics, descriptions of games and projects, and worship materials appear throughout the book with some additional resources in the final section. All of them can be reproduced for use with the youth in your church. Permission must be requested to photocopy materials for other purposes. A cross-referenced index is included at the back of the book.

We hope this book will help you create meaningful and spirited programs for your youth group. May the Spirit guide you in this challenging, fun, and important ministry!

Planning and Implementing Youth Programs

The Developmental Needs of Youth

Many books give detailed information about the developmental stages of youth and the implications of these for youth ministry. In their research for "Young Adolescents and Their Communities: A Shared Responsibility," William Kerewsky and Leah M. Lefstein* suggest that young people have the following seven developmental needs:

- Competence and achievement
- Creative expression
- Meaningful participation
- Physical activity
- Positive social interaction with peers and adults
- Self-definition
- Structure and clear limits.

Kerewsky and Lefstein acknowledge the enormous developmental diversity among young adolescents. They conclude that youth require a variety of types and levels of activities designed to meet these seven needs. Few youth programs can meet all seven needs at once. Recognizing this, Kerewsky and Lefstein suggest planning programs that meet a minimum of four developmental needs in each program, and trying to vary these four from program to program.

* From *3:00 to 6:00 P.M.: Young Adolescents at Home in the Community* (Carrboro: University of North Carolina, 1982)

Youth and the Learning Process

Learning usually follows a sequential process. You have an experience, you reflect on it, and you try to integrate the newly gained knowledge into your life. As Christians, we know we are never alone in this process. God is part of all our learning.

The **Idea Pages** in this book include ideas for creating programs based on this learning process (an "action-reflection-integration" model). Each **Idea Page** includes suggestions for the following five program elements:

1. Check-in

The starting point in the learning process consists of a person's life experiences, knowledge, talents, values, and needs. We are more likely to provide programs that meet the needs and interests of our group members if we have some understanding of their physical, spiritual, emotional, and social development. Some of this may come from reading books. Most of it will come from personal relationships with the youth in your group. A check-in process can help both leaders and group members "tune in" to one another after being apart. It can also help to integrate newcomers. The objectives of a check-in activity are to hear from everyone, to learn from everyone, and to get to know each other better. Sometimes the check-in requires a response to a question. Ideally,

everyone – including the leader – responds. In order to create a safe environment, everyone should also have the "right to pass," that is, the right to say nothing if they wish.

2. Experiences

Both the planned and the unexpected, the "good break" and the "stroke of bad luck," provide significant experiences in our lives. They spark change and growth in us. Young people can have significant experiences during retreats, Bible study, service projects, a closing meditation, and in their everyday lives – with an unusual dream, the death of a friend, an award for personal achievement. As leaders, we can create opportunities for youth to have experiences that will encourage spiritual growth. We can also design youth programs that respond to the day-to-day experiences of concern to our members. Be open and flexible, ready to adapt activities to suit your group.

3. Reflection

Reflection involves analyzing and reflecting on our experiences. It may involve gathering more information or having another experi-ence. Reflection can include solitary activities like praying, guided meditation, and journal writing, as well as interactive situations like small group discussions, role plays, and research. People gain insights by reflecting on experiences. These may come as a sudden "aha!" during the experience or they may develop slowly.

4. Integration

Integration involves applying new learning by doing. Through self-expression, youth make the connection between their new insights and their day-to-day realities. In planning youth pro-grams, we can select activities like projects, games, and crafts to help youth apply their faith discoveries to their everyday lives.

5. Closing Worship

In worship, youth have opportunities to recog-nize and feel God's presence in their lives. Worship can include scripture, prayer, music, and rituals. You may want to have worship at the beginning, the end, or at both times in your program.

Designing Youth Programs

With the learning process as a guideline and the **Idea Pages** as a resource, we can design programs that meet the developmental needs of our group members.

IdeaPage

We suggest following these steps:

1. Choose an Idea Page theme for the program and decide on your program goals.

2. Decide how to do the "Group Check-In." Use the one suggested on the Idea Page, adapt it, or substitute another.

3. Choose activities from the Idea Page for each of these learning stages:

   Experience

   Reflection

   Integration

4. Add a couple of the group's favorite games or other activities that relate to the theme.

5. Include a worship. Each Idea Page has suggestions for "Closing Worship"* that can be adapted to begin or end your program.

6. Review your whole program outline to confirm that the activities meet at least four developmental needs. If you are not satisfied, consider ways to adapt activities.

*Add your own musical options to the worship (and to other parts of the program), drawing on the traditions of your denomination.

A blank outline follows for you to copy and use for designing your own programs. When you review your program outline, check off the needs that the program will meet. After every youth group meeting or event, take a moment to evaluate what happened, noting comments on the form. After several weeks, look back over these forms and ask these questions:

• Do the programs I design meet the same developmental needs each time?

• If so, which needs am I ignoring? How can I meet these needs?

• Do I need to adapt activities more often to meet specific needs of members in this group?

Use your evaluation comments and your answers to these questions to help you improve the design of future programs.

PROGRAM OUTLINE

GROUP NAME:

DATE:

THEME:

GOALS:

Group Check-in:

Experience:	**Needed:**
Reflection:	**Needed:**
Integration:	**Needed:**
Other:	**Needed:**
Closing Worship:	**Needed:**

This program addresses these developmental needs:

○ physical activity
○ competence and achievement
○ self-definition
○ creative expression
○ positive social interaction
○ structure and clear limits
○ meaningful participation

Getting Your Group Off the Ground

Whether starting up a new group or bringing youth back together, take time to think about how you will contact individuals. Are there one or two key youth who are willing and available to work with you to get the group going? Ask for their ideas and their help. Together collect the names and addresses of all potential group members. Ask for names from your clergy, church school leaders, church directory, and from young people themselves. Send out invitations to everyone on your list. Then follow up with a phone call personally inviting them to the first group meeting. Encourage everyone to bring along friends.

For your first meeting, plan a non-threatening social gathering – one where youth will feel comfortable bringing along their friends. They will also find it easier to get to know one another. Plan the event for early autumn when young people are deciding which extracurricular activities, sports teams, and groups they want to join.

Take time in the first few weeks to brainstorm some activities and topics the youth are interested in. Use the Vital Statistics form on page 14.

Advertise! Advertise! Advertise!

Be creative in your advertising. Use lots of graphics, including those found in this book. Ask permission to put up posters at local schools and places where youth gather in your community. Advertise on a television station that gives free space to community groups.

If your church puts out a newsletter or personal letter from the clergy before the end of the summer, or has a home page on the Internet, include information about the youth group and its programs. Set up an information table in the narthex or church hall after worship. Display information and pictures of the youth group from previous years.

The key is lots of visibility and lots of advertising – at the start-up and throughout the year.

Group Standards

Each youth needs to feel that he or she is safe emotionally and physically when in this group. Early in the year, take time to consider what behaviors will create a climate of trust and acceptance for everyone. We recommend these three essential ingredients: 1. No put-downs (everyone has the right to respect) 2. The right to pass (the right to speak and the right not to speak) 3. "What we say here stays here" (the right to confidentiality). Talk about these three standards and others that are important to group members. List them on paper and post them. Additionally, you might have all youth sign their names to this page to show their commitment to abide by the group standards. Group members should take responsibility for explaining them to newcomers and visitors.

Building Relationships with Youth Group Members

Often we make a difference in the lives of young people through the personal relationships we build with them. Our concern, our willingness to listen, and the interest we take in their lives can have an affirming and lasting impression. How do youth leaders build and maintain relationships with group members throughout the year? Keeping in touch with youth takes an investment of time and energy, but it is a key component in youth ministry. Here are suggestions to help you.

• **Phone regularly.** Despite the popularity of e-mail, the telephone is still a teenager's favorite mode of communication. Sometimes you may need to make phone calls to remind youth of group plans or to bring something. These provide opportunities to connect with members. Call on birthdays, when someone has been absent, or just to say "hi." Remember – you don't always need a reason for calling.

• **Keep notes.** Write the name, address, birth date, and telephone number of each group member on a recipe card along with any known interests or hobbies. Keep these updated. When you have a telephone conversation, have the person's card in front of you. For example, if a youth tells you they are preparing for a difficult exam, write this down. The next time you call, follow up with them by asking about the exam. Be sure you keep all information confidential.

- **Show interest.** Attend a drama, sporting game, band concert, etc. in which youth are involved. Remember to phone them afterward to let them know what you thought of it. Visit their place of employment (and be a paying customer!). Clip out news/publicize recognition that youth have received from other groups, institutions, or agencies. Display these on a bulletin board.

- **Recognize and encourage talents.** Suggest volunteer or paid opportunities for leadership that match the interests and skills of individual youth. Encourage them to "go for it" and offer to write a letter of reference!

- **Send postcards.** When you're away on holidays, send postcards to the youth in your group. Over the summer, encourage the youth to keep in touch with you by sending postcards from places they visit. Make a display of these at the end of the summer.

- **Publish a newsletter.** Send out a regular newsletter that lets youth know about upcoming events and describes things you've done as a group. Include lots of graphics and cartoons. Invite youth to contribute their own art. Encourage them to let their families read the newsletter, too.

- **Prepare monthly calendars.** Photocopy the Youth Events Calendar on page 15. Record the meeting times and dates, group members' birthdays, and upcoming special events. Make copies for group members. Encourage the youth to put these on the refrigerator door so their parents will also have this information.

- **Recognize birthdays.** Recognize birthdays, graduations, and other milestones. Phone youth or send a card on their birthdays. Find free electronic greetings at www.egreetings.com, www.shoebox.com, or www.bluemountain.com. Or plan as a group to recognize birthdays. At the beginning of the year ask each member if they want to buy a small gift under five dollars, wrap it, and put it in a "birthday box." When someone has a birthday they choose a gift from the box. Or youth might agree to bake birthday cakes. When the first member of the group has a birthday someone agrees to bake a cake. The person who had the birthday cake baked for them provides the cake for the next birthday, and so on. Be sure to recognize in some way the birthdays that happen over the summer.

- **Organize special outings.** A meeting away from the church – to watch a movie, go bowling, swimming, or a fundraising project – provides an opportunity for youth to relax and enjoy getting to know each other in a different setting. See fundraising ideas on pages 124-125.

- **Pastoral support.** Acknowledge the loss of people close to them. Youth are often overlooked when a family member, such as a grandparent, dies. Visit them in their home or seek them out at the memorial service. Don't be afraid to ask questions and talk about the deceased person.

Youth Vital Statistics

Name _____   Address _____

Phone _____   E-mail address _____

Birth date _____   Age _____   Grade _____

Allergies_____

☑ **Check all that apply to you.**

Some things I would be interested in doing this year:

❑ Crafts – Examples:_____
_____
_____

❑ Participate in a worship service
❑ Attend a service in another church (or other denomination)
❑ Baking or cooking
❑ Journaling/creative writing
❑ Drama/acting
❑ Playing active games
❑ Playing board/card games (e.g. Bible trivia)
❑ Watch videos
❑ Have a meal together
❑ Have a prayer vigil (e.g. all night Saturday to Sunday)
❑ Have a sleepover

My other great ideas are:

_____
_____
_____

Some topics I would be interested in discussing:

❑ Relationships
❑ What other religions/churches believe
❑ Influence of media/advertising
❑ Mystical topics (e.g. angels, dreams/visions, life after death)

❑ Self-esteem/identity issues
❑ Suicide
❑ Abuse of scripture (e.g. slavery, homophobia, oppression of women)
❑ Sexuality
❑ Cults/the occult
❑ How the Bible came to be (e.g. Who wrote it? When?)

My other great ideas are:

_____
_____
_____

I'd be willing to help in the group in the following ways:

❑ Lead a discussion
❑ Write an opening/closing prayer
❑ Read scripture
❑ Lead a prayer/meditation
❑ Driving (myself/my parents available)
❑ Typing/stuff on the computer

Overall, I would have to say I think the Bible is:

❑ Boring
❑ A mystery to me
❑ Relevant (i.e. has something to say)
❑ Long!
❑ Irrelevant (i.e. has nothing to say to me)
❑ Interesting

Youth Events Calendar

Five Signs of a Healthy Youth Group

Lots of churches consider the size of a group the measure of whether it is a healthy group. How many times, when evaluating an event, activity, or program, has the first question asked been, "How many kids came?" This approach is understandable; after all, numbers are tangible, concrete, and measurable. Numbers don't lie – but do they tell the whole truth? As Frank Mercadante says in *Growing Teen Disciples* (Indiana: Ave Maria Press, 1998), "If numbers are a measure of success, then we must concede that Jesus was somewhat of a failure. Jesus' own ministry numbers seemed to fluctuate. His miracles and healings seemed to draw huge crowds. But when he taught hard things (like death and resurrection) his popularity waned. In the end everyone abandoned him, including his closest followers...Numbers were never Jesus' bottom line." If numbers aren't the sign that a group is healthy, what is?

1. The programs facilitate the relationships, not the other way around.

Let's face it, years from now, what the youth are going to remember aren't all the things you did or what they learned. What they remember are the people, especially the significant adults who made a difference in their lives. As William Meyers says in his book *Theological Themes of Youth Ministry* (New York: The Pilgrim Press, 1987), "All the fancy programs, the resources, the buildings, and the ski trips cannot replace the essential starting point – the presence of faithful adults who incarnate good news by their very presence." This "people first" approach to youth ministry doesn't mean that programs aren't important. The purpose of the program ideas in this book is to create an atmosphere of trust and acceptance in which to build relationships.

2. The leaders are "people of the way" – people who see themselves as on a path or faith journey.

We cannot take a young person where we have never journeyed ourselves. Disciples make disciples.

Youth leaders must be what William Meyers calls *guarantors*. A guarantor is someone who is appropriately anchored in adulthood, but who will walk with youth on their journey. He writes that "adolescents, both churched and non-churched, move into and through the wilderness, often inadequately armed and yet in hopeful search of guides, beacons, and known pathways." This does not imply that we have all the answers. It means that we are spiritually healthy, open, and growing.

3. The group is connected to the wider congregation.

Youth *ministry* isn't just a fancy term for youth group. Ministry with and for youth may include youth group, religious education programs, confirmation classes, summer camp, and weekly worship. In carrying out its ministry to youth, congregations will acknowledge and offer pastoral care to youth who have lost someone close to them or when parents divorce. Ministry to youth recognizes accomplishments and milestones in a youth's life, such as graduation. Making funds available for youth to attend a youth conference or event is another way a congregation ministers to youth. The sign of a healthy group is one that is a well-integrated part of the larger ministry of the whole congregation to youth and their families.

This book contains many suggestions for ways youth can participate in the service and fellowship of the congregation. It is structured according to the seasons of the Church Year in the hopes that leaders will find ways to involve the youth in planning and participating in congregational activities such as Advent parties, Holy Week activities, and worship services.

4. Worship is a key component.

In *Theological Themes in Youth Ministry*, William Meyers describes worship in the context of youth ministry as "that occasion when sacred space is intentionally sought by ritual elders." (Meyers uses the term *ritual elders* to describe adult believers.) How do we intentionally seek sacred space? Through prayer, ritual, guided meditation, even silence. As youth leaders, we cannot *make* spiritual experiences, but we can create the sacred space in which they might happen.

Each Idea Page in this book includes a suggestion for a closing moment of worship, as well as resources for retreats, an Easter Vigil, and other special times of worship throughout the year.

5. The group is a safe place.

A healthy group takes seriously the need to create a place where youth feel safe – both physically and emotionally. Churches approach this in different ways: by requiring two leaders, by balancing leadership with a male and female leader, by requiring a criminal records check be done on all those who have contact with youth and children, and by hiring leaders who demonstrate healthy boundaries. Members can also take responsibility for ensuring the group is a safe place for everyone by agreeing to group standards of behavior.

Videos and Youth Groups

Videos can be wonderful learning tools and great discussion starters for youth. Careful preparation and planning ensure their effectiveness. Build in program time not only for viewing the video, but also for debriefing and discussing issues raised by it. This is particularly critical if the movie explores difficult or disturbing subject matter. Extend the normal program time to allow for this. Feature-length films are usually too long to view and discuss in a regular-length program. Incorporate viewing and discussing a film into a sleepover or evening at a youth group member's home; or choose to show only a clip of the video to start discussion (especially if this is a movie many of the youth have already seen).

Commercially sold films and videos from rental outlets* are licensed "for home use only." A church, or anywhere other than a private home, is considered a "public place." Showing them in such places violates the law. Some church youth groups have been fined. For more information about copyright laws, visit one of the websites listed on this page.

You can show these videos outside of the home only with permission from the copyright holder or film distributor. You may gain permission from the distributor by phoning them directly, or by purchasing a license from a motion picture licensing company. If your church has an adult video discussion group, several youth groups, and church school classes that like to use videos, you may want to explore this option. In Canada, contact **Audio Cine Films** toll free at 1-800-289-8887 or visit their website at http://www.acf-film.com. ACF represents many production companies including Disney, Warner Bros., Universal, Alliance, Paramount, MGM, Miramax, and Orion. In the US, the **Motion Picture Licensing Corporation** (http://www.mplc.com) has begun a new cooperative venture with **Christian Video Licensing International**, offering licenses to churches that cover many production companies including Disney, Trimark, Warner Bros., Touchstone, MGM, Buena Vista and many religious video distributors. You can reach them toll free at 1-888-771-2854 or through their website at http://www.cvli.org.

*Videos rented or purchased from church outlets, which are licensed for educational use, do not carry these restrictions.

Section A: Season after Pentecost

Mood and Flavor of the Season

The Season after Pentecost is the longest season in the Christian Year. It stretches from Pentecost Sunday in late May or early June to Reign of Christ Sunday at the end of November. During this time we celebrate the growth of the church after Pentecost. We also explore how we can be the hands and feet of Christ, carrying on his work in the world. The liturgical color of the season is green, symbolizing growth.

Scripture readings during this season have a strong social justice flavor, calling us to live with concern for our neighbor. In the Season after Pentecost we take time to dream of a world of wholeness, harmony, and peace; we imagine God's reign of shalom happening in today's world. We reflect on how we live in community, how we accept and support one another, and how we grow together in God's way.

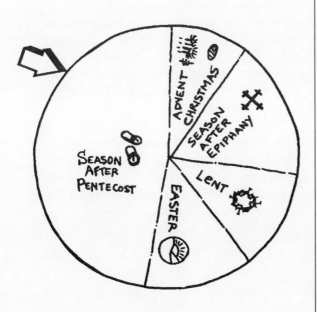

Special Days

In autumn we think about Thanksgiving Sunday, but there are other special days. Christians around the world celebrate Worldwide Communion Sunday on the first Sunday of October. World Food Day is October 16. October 24 marks the anniversary of the United Nations and the start of Disarmament Week. Peace Sabbath also falls in October. Many of these special days reflect the themes of Jubilee (see next page). September 11 marks the anniversary of the terrorist attacks in the United States. Remembrance or Veterans' Day is November 11 and the month of November is Holocaust Month. November 9–10 marks the anniversary of *Kristallnacht* (Crystal Night), or "The Night of the Broken Glass." On this night, in 1938, the German army set fire to synagogues, looted and destroyed hundreds of Jewish-owned stores and homes in cities and towns all over Germany. More than 1,000 Jews were killed and 30,000 others were arrested and sent to concentration camps.

These special days are not part of the Christian Year, but many churches recognize them as expressions of our vision and commitment as Christians.

The liturgical festival of All Saints also occurs during this season. All Saints is a time when we celebrate our participation in the Communion of Saints, that great company of Christian believers, past and present. The Feast of All Saints dates back to the fifth century when the church dedicated a day to the memory of all the Christian martyrs who had been killed for their faith. Until then, the early church had remembered each martyr on a particular day of the year, but soon there were more martyrs than days in the year. It was also recognized

that many martyrs and saints were unknown and uncelebrated. This feast was for them too. Originally, the saints were honored and remembered as part of the joyful celebrations of the Easter season. In the Eastern Church the saints are still remembered at this time, but in 844 Pope Gregory IV moved All Saints' Day to November 1 for the Western Church. Hallowe'en, or All Hallows' Eve, is a part of the three-day celebration that includes All Hallows' Eve, All Saints' Day, and All Souls' Day. Hallowe'en began as a secular holiday, a Celtic festival to mark the end of the old year. It was believed that the spirits of the dead visited their homes at this time and that unfriendly spirits roamed the earth, creating mischief. Hallowe'en costumes began to appear in medieval times when it was customary for churches to display the relics of the martyred saints; those parishes too poor to have relics let parishioners dress up to imitate the saints.

The Season after Pentecost ends with Reign of Christ Sunday. On this last Sunday in the Christian Year we commit ourselves again to work for God's reign in our world. Your group might hold a New (church) Year's Eve party on Reign of Christ Sunday (see ideas for an Advent Party on page 40). This is a fun way to put emphasis on the Christian Year, rather than on the celebration of the secular one.

What is Jubilee?

The word "Jubilee" appears in three places in the Bible, but primarily in  chapters 25 and 27 of the Book of Leviticus. Jubilee is an all-encompassing vision of social and ecological justice that calls for release from bondage, redistribution of wealth, and renewal of the earth. In the biblical tradition, a Sabbath year was declared every seventh year. A Jubilee Year occurred every seven Sabbath years, or every 50 years. In the year

of Jubilee, slaves were to be set free, debts were to be forgiven, wealth was to be equitably shared among all, and the land was to be given rest from its labor. Jubilee is a call that is echoed elsewhere in the Hebrew Scriptures and which is central to Jesus' ministry to "bring good news to the poor...to proclaim release to the captives and...to let the oppressed go free" (Luke 4:18). Although there is no real proof that a Jubilee ever occurred, the ideal is a hopeful one. As we enter the third millennium, our world is also in need of a hopeful vision to address debt, unjust working conditions, poverty, and environmental crises of the 21st century.

Implications for Youth Ministry

The mood and flavor of the Season after Pentecost suggest many rich themes and program possibilities.

The theme of community is an important one for youth groups, especially at this time of year when most groups are beginning. This season provides opportunities to build community within your own group as well as within the larger community. Doing projects together, perhaps focusing on the issues of world hunger, disarmament, and peace, can help build a sense of community in your group. At the same time these projects can benefit the larger community.

As groups are forming, youth need to get to know one another and to develop a sense of group identity. Group members may play name games and trust exercises, create some group "standards" of behavior, and plan future programs together (see page 12 for a description of group standards).

The Idea Pages in this section include suggestions to help you build a sense of belonging and community in your group. Take time to build relationships of trust between group members – these will create the foundation on which you build programs for the rest of the year.

Building Community

Group Check-in

You will need: name tags cut from various colors of construction paper. Ask youth to choose a name tag of a favorite color and write on their name tag their favorite vacation spot, subject in school, Bible person, the number of siblings they have, and the place they were born, along with their name. Use this as an ice-breaker. For example, invite the youth to find someone who likes the same school subject and to discuss with their partner why they like it. Or find someone with the same number of siblings; describe your siblings to your partner.

People Bingo

This game is a great mixer and a fun way for group members to learn more about each other.

Instructions: Copy the blank **Bingo Card** on page 114. Write descriptive phrases in the squares such as "Has been in a musical/play" or "Has seen Phantom Menace" or "Has their epidermis showing (oooh!)", leaving room in each square for a signature. Make photocopies of the filled-in card. Hand out copies of the Bingo card and pencils. Invite group members to find people who fit these descriptions and get their signatures. (Group members shouldn't sign their own cards.) Encourage them to get as many signatures as possible and to fill in every box. Stop the activity when someone has filled in their entire card. Read out the descriptions and find out who fits each one. Several people may fit each description.

Youth Vital Statistics

If this is the first time you are meeting, and especially if this is a new group, ask group members to fill out a sheet with their "vital stats." Use the **Vital Stats** card provided on page 14 or create your own. Use these to gather basic information such as phone number, birth date, and e-mail address, as well as gauging needs and interest in types of activities.

Who are you?

The object of this game is to get to know people's names.

Instructions: You will need one fewer chair than you have people. One person stands in the middle. The middle person points to a circle member and says, "Who are you?" That person responds with their name. The middle person then asks that same circle member, "Who are your neighbors?" The person responds with the names of the people on their right and left. If the circle member doesn't know the names, then they go to the middle. If the circle member does know the names, the middle person asks, "Who else would you like to know?" The person then says something like "All those people with white socks on." All the people with white socks on would have to get up and find another seat and the middle person also tries to claim a seat. The person left without a seat stands in the center of the circle and play continues.

Multiple Handshakes

This game works best with larger groups.

Instructions: The game leader whispers a number in each person's ear. Everyone then walks around shaking hands with whomever they meet. All the 1s will shake once, the 2s will shake twice, and the 3s will shake three times. When they find someone with the same number they introduce themselves by name and share one thing about themselves (e.g. what school they attend, what their middle name is, a favorite pastime).

Tossing Out Names

A good way to get to know each other's names.

Instructions: Stand in a circle. One person starts by calling out their own name and then tossing a ball to another person in the circle. That person calls out their own name and tosses the ball to someone else. This continues until everyone has had several chances to catch the ball and say their own name. Then, play the game again but this time the person tossing the ball calls out the name of the person who is to catch it. To make it more challenging, gradually add more balls (depending on the size of the group).

Lap to Lap

This game works with groups of any size.

Instructions: Everyone sits on chairs in a circle. The game leader asks all those with a particular characteristic to move a specific number of seats to the right or left, and to sit down on the lap of whomever is sitting there. For example, the leader might say, "If you came to youth group today in a car, get up and move 2 chairs to the right and sit down." Some other examples:

- If you like pizza with pineapple on it
- If you are wearing jeans
- If you are wearing something that belongs to someone else
- If you have seen a movie this week
- If you haven't moved yet

Quick Change

This game works best with larger groups.

Instructions: You will need one fewer chair than you have people. Everyone sits on chairs in a circle. The person without a chair stands in the middle and calls out an instruction such as "All those who ate cereal for breakfast change seats." Once they have called out the instruction, those who fit the description stand up and move quickly to a vacant seat. The person in the middle also tries to find a seat. Whoever is left without a seat gives the next instruction. Some other examples:

- All those who have shoes with shoelaces change seats.
- All those who have a birthday in May change seats.
- All those who have a nickname change seats.
- All those who have brown eyes change seats.

I Have Never…

This is a good game for small groups.

You will need: a large bowl and stir sticks or toothpicks
Instructions: The group sits in a circle with a large bowl in the middle. Each person in the group receives 10 stir sticks or toothpicks. Choose someone to begin the game. This person should say things such as "I have never gone horseback riding" or "I have never played Play-station" or "I have never read the *Cat in the Hat*." All the people in the group that have done the "I have never…" action must put a stick in the bowl. Rule: The "I have never…" statements cannot be sexually explicit.

Zip, Zap, Zoom

This is a quick name game.

Instructions: The group forms a circle with one person in the middle. The person in the middle points to a person in the circle and says either *"ZIP," "ZAP" or "ZOOM."* "Zip" means the person to your right. "Zap" means the person to your left. "Zoom" means you. If the person in the middle counts to 10 before the other person can say the name, then the person pointed to is in the middle. If they say the name before the person in the middle finishes counting to 10, then they try again.

Group Building a Snack

You will need: a variety of food items (such as sultanas, almonds, chocolate, sunflower seeds, pretzels) to create "trail mix"
Group members should work together to create a snack that will be enjoyed by all. Check first for allergies and do not include these items. While enjoying the snack, discuss how members have different likes and dislikes and how you will work together to create a group where everyone's needs are considered. You may want to create some group standards of behavior (see page 12 for a description).

Additional resources
Energizers and Other Great Cooperative Activities for All Ages by Carol Apacki (Granville, OH: Quest Books, 1991).

Closing Worship

Join hands in a circle. One person in the circle drops the hand of the person on their left. While still holding the hand of the person on their right, they begin to walk around the outside of the circle. The person whose hand was dropped stays still while the rest follow the first person. The spiral will get tighter and tighter. To unwind, the person in the middle crawls out, still holding one hand, and the rest follow.

Prayer:
God of love, we know that you love us.
As we gather together, help us to remember your love for each one of us,
so that in what we do and say we may respect and value everyone here,
including ourselves. Amen.

Cooperation and Trust

Group Check-in

Create a masking tape line on the floor long enough to allow the whole group to stand on it. Begin by inviting everyone to get on the "log." When everyone is on the log, ask them to rearrange themselves, according to their height, without stepping off the log. If a person falls off the log, the group must start over. Repeat the exercise several times having the youth line up: alphabetically according to the first letter of their name, by month in which they were born, by age or grade, by number of people in their family, etc.

Spin-off "Survivor" Game

Begin by sitting in a circle, perhaps around a campfire made from logs, with tissue paper and a flashlight to simulate the fire. You might even play the *Survivor* soundtrack or a tape of nature sounds to set the mood. Invite someone to describe the popular TV series *Survivor*. (A group of 16 people were selected to live on a deserted island/the Australian Outback for 42 days. They were given tasks they had to work together to complete. Each week a contestant was "voted off" the show. The last person who remained won a million dollars.) Explain that unlike the TV show where group members compete with each other for the prize, they must work together to complete tasks as a team. Team members should encourage each other by clapping, cheering, and offering help as needed. Each time the team completes a task they return to the circle to await the next instructions. Give all instructions before they move to an activity. Some examples of group tasks:

• **Balloon Relay** – Each person gets a balloon. Group members line up at one end of a room (i.e. the starting line). One person begins by blowing up their balloon (but not tying it!). They then let the balloon go. Wherever the deflated balloon lands, the player rushes over, picks up the balloon, blows it up, and repeats, until they reach the far end of the room. Then they pick up their balloon and run back to the starting line. The next player blows up their balloon, lets it deflate, moves forward, and so on – until all team members have returned to the starting line.

• **Stepping Stones** – Imagine the floor is quicksand. The only way to get across is by stepping on stones. Group members line up at one end of a room (i.e. the starting line). Give the first person in line two paper plates and demonstrate how to walk by laying down one "stone", stepping on it, then laying down the other stone close to the first one and stepping to it, and so on.

• **Catching Fish** – It's time for dinner and the team must catch some fish to eat! Scatter fish (cotton balls) around the room. Use masking tape to create the outline of a net on the floor. Give each person a drinking straw. Team members must work together to blow all the fish into the net.

• **Night Hike** – The team must make a dangerous trip through the jungle at night. To ensure everyone arrives safely at the destination, they must stay connected. Have group members join hands in a circle and travel some distance without releasing hands. (They must remain in a circle or else the people on the ends are vulnerable.) Make this difficult by instructing them to move from one room to another through a doorway, or maneuver around chairs or under tables while staying connected. Leaders might pose as predators, trying to break into the circle to drag someone off. Set a time limit for completing the trip to add to the tension.

• **Skill Challenge** – Place a quarter in a bucket that contains at least 12 in. (30 cm) of water. Give the team 50 pennies. The object of the game is to drop pennies into the water and try to completely cover the quarter. Teams can decide how they will work together to do this – by taking turns, or electing the person with the steadiest hand, etc.

• **Hauling Water** – You need lots of fresh water to survive on an island. Group members line up at one end of a room (i.e. the starting line). The first two people must get to the other end of the room and back balancing a paper cup full of water between them. The cup might be balanced between elbows, backs, on arms, etc. but it must be balanced (not held). If they drop the cup they must return to the starting line and begin again. Once they have reached the other end of the room and have returned to the starting line, they pour the water (or what's left of it!) into a container. The next two people start with another full cup. The pair may decide to carry (balance) it a different way or the same way.

Discuss:

- What is it like to play games that encourage participation without emphasis on competing to win?

- How were the feelings you had during the game different or similar to your feelings when you play competitive games?

- How do you think competitiveness affects a group? What are both positive and negative aspects of competition among people?

- What kind of group will this be? How will we ensure that everyone can and does participate?

Frozen Shoe

Everyone removes their shoes. Each person moves around the room while balancing one of their shoes, upside down, on the top of their head. Players are not allowed to touch the shoe with their hands. If the shoe falls off, the person is frozen until a friend picks up the shoe and puts it back on that person's head, making sure that their own shoe stays balanced.

Zoom

Zany and loud fun for groups of any size!

Instructions: Stand close to each other in a circle. Pass the word "Zoom" around the circle, from person to person (i.e. each person repeats the word "zoom"). It will probably go slowly at first (like first gear in a car). Ask the group to try a little faster – second gear, then third gear, then overdrive! Finally, the leader applies the brakes by sticking out a leg on an imaginary brake pedal. As soon as the rest of the group sees this action they must all yell "Screech!" Take turns applying the brakes. Try "reversing" around the circle, saying the word "Mooz" faster and faster until someone applies the brakes.

Human Twister

Begin by having group members link arms. The object of the game is for the group to work as one body. As in the game of Twister®, the leader calls out instructions such as "Put your right hand on something pink" or "Put your left foot on something white" or "Touch your head to something black." Only one person in the group needs to do this, as all the others are attached to the "body." However, once a group member has placed their hand/foot etc. on a color, they cannot remove it. So the group should work together to decide who is the best person to follow the instruction. This game takes some maneuvering and stretching! The game ends when someone is no longer able to hold their position.

Closing Worship

Trace and cut out the outline of a body from newsprint. As part of your closing, invite group members to write their names on the paper. Read 1 Corinthians 12:12–27.

Prayer:
Draw close to us, O God,
as we gather in this group.
Help us to see you in one another.
Help us to hear your voice in all we say and do.
Amen.

Jubilee: Freedom from Slavery

Group Check-in

Choose a breakfast cereal that describes what you are like. Take turns explaining your choice to the other group members (e.g. "I am most like Rice Krispies, because I have a 'snap, crackle, and pop' personality").

Jubilee: Lifting the Burden of Debt

Jubilee is an all-encompassing vision of social and ecological justice that calls for release from bondage, redistribution of wealth, and renewal of the earth. In the biblical text, *release from bondage* referred to both the forgiveness of debilitating debts and the release of slaves. Although these problems take a different form today than they did in the Israelites' time, they are still with us. Examples of contemporary bondage include the problem of sex-trade workers in South Asia, exploitative working conditions, and the debt crisis in the developing world.

What's Behind a Label?

Ask participants to help each other read the label on their shirts to find out where the clothing was made. List the countries on a sheet of newsprint. Together brainstorm what the group knows about these countries (e.g. climate, economic status, population, history, politics). You may want to locate these countries on an atlas or globe.

Sweatshop Simulation Exercise

Instructions: Prepare 4 envelopes according to instructions (see box). On a sheet of newsprint, draw the following shapes and their values: square ($50), triangle ($20), circle ($10), rectangle ($1).

> **Envelope #1** (Canada/US): 20 pieces of paper, 5 pencils, 5 pair of scissors, 5 rulers, compass.
>
> **Envelope #2** (Taiwan/Korea): 8 pieces of paper, 1 pencil, 2 pair of scissors, (no ruler).
>
> **Envelope #3** (Mexico): 10 pieces of paper, 3 pencils, 3 pair of scissors, 1 ruler.
>
> **Envelope #4** (Guatemala/Honduras): 3 pieces of paper, 1 pair of scissors (no ruler or pencils).

To play the game: Divide participants into 4 groups. Give each group an envelope and explain the instructions.

Instructions:

1. Each group represents a country and your objective is to use the materials in your envelope and your own ingenuity to create "products" (squares, triangles, circles, etc.) at the designated values.

2. Exact measurements are required. You may measure the shapes on the newsprint but must not trace these.

3. You can talk.

4. You have 10 minutes to create as many products as you can.

While groups are working, the game leader notes any comments or reactions – for example, if a group tries to cheat or steal from another group, purchase or trade supplies, or complains about things not being fair. After 5 minutes call a stop to all activity. Then allow the groups from Taiwan/Korea and Guatemala/Honduras to work for 5 more minutes. Continue to note comments and reactions. At the end of 10 minutes the game is over. Teams should bring their products to you to tally up their scores. Reject anything that is not exact in measurements. Use your discretion to accept or reject shapes that have ragged edges or are torn.

Debrief using the following questions.

- What is the value of the goods your group produced? If you divided this amongst group members, what are the earnings per person?

- How much "resources" (i.e. paper) did you start with? How did this affect the outcome? How did the tools (i.e. pencils, scissors, etc.) you had to work with affect the outcome?

- How much "labor" (i.e. persons on your team) did you have? How much of it did you use? How was it used? How did this affect the outcome?

- How much of your resources did you waste?

- What do you notice about how this compares to other countries? What does this represent about countries of the developing world and the industrialized world?

- How did you feel about some teams getting more time to work than others? What do you think this represents (e.g. longer working hours in Third World countries, lack of labor laws to protect workers, large but unskilled labor pool)?

- The game leader should share any observations they made during the exercise. For example, if a team gave up or tried to steal or trade for resources or tools. Or if a wealthier country was unwilling to share its resources or skills.

Share information about sweatshops (e.g. maquiladoras) and labor practices in the developing world. See **Additional Resources** for website addresses and suggested films.

Sweatshop Fashion Show

Hold a sweatshop fashion show at your church. Group members should wear clothing made by both retailers who are violators and those who have adopted "codes of conduct." Research companies and their business practices and use these to write "runway commentaries" (e.g. Jane is wearing a lovely ensemble of black jeans and long-sleeved shirt designed by Levi Strauss, white Nike Air Essentials, and she finishes it all off with a smart messenger bag and black beanie from the GAP. The shoes are manufactured in Indonesia where women work 10 to 12 hours a day for US$2.46 to create shoes that retail for $65 a pair.) Youth can take turns being both models and commentators. You might serve tea and dessert; money raised could be donated to an organization working for fair labor conditions in the garment industry. Have petitions on hand for people to sign. (Also see the description of an Alternatives Fair on page 28 for a way to raise funds to support producers and artisans in developing countries.

Global Breakfast Cereal Exercise

You will need: a variety of breakfast cereal boxes
Ask youth to name their favorite breakfast cereals. Then look at the examples you have brought. Read the ingredients and see if you can determine from where in our world these ingredients might have come. For example, Harvest Crunch contains rolled oats and whole wheat (Canada), brown sugar (Trinidad), raisins (Spain), coconut (Samoa), dates (Lebanon) and almonds (Italy). List countries on newsprint.

Some countries in our world export food even though many people in those countries don't have enough to eat. Why do you think that is (e.g. the countries need cash in order to pay off their loans/debts)? Identify which of the countries you've listed are among the 50 most highly indebted countries in the world. Talk about how the Jubilee movement is calling for debt relief for these countries and about how your group might help.

Poverty Awareness Meal

Host a poverty awareness meal. Invite congregation members to forego a complete meal that night. Serve soup, crackers, and tea or coffee. Suggest that participants contribute what they would have paid for a full meal in a restaurant and dedicate the offering to your denomination's world hunger relief program.

Use the dinner hour to become more aware of the fact that over half the world goes to bed hungry every night. Share a documentary film about the reality of poverty in our world. End the evening with Communion and include prayers of thanksgiving, confession, and intercession. Encourage people to go to bed without a snack.

Additional resources

http://www.corpwatch.org Corporate Watch
http://www.maquilasolidarity.org The Maquila Solidarity Network
http://www.sweatshopwatch.org Sweatshop Watch
http://www.web.net/~tendays/youth.html Ten Days for Global Justice
http://www.cleanclothes.org Clean Clothes Campaign
http://www.adbusters.org Adbusters
http://www.dropthedebt.org Drop the Debt

Closing Worship

Prayer:
Liberating God,
help us to be inspired by the vision of Jubilee,
to imagine a new beginning,
to seek justice,
to disturb the rich,
to challenge the powerful,
to stand with the poor,
so that we may live the Jubilee in our place and time. Amen.

Jubilee: Redistribution of Wealth

Idea Page

Group Check-in

Invite group members to come up with a newspaper headline to sum up something that happened in their life last week. The headline might reflect something interesting they did, some good news they received, or something that had an effect on them. Have group members yell, "Extra! Extra! Read all about it..." and then have group members take turns shouting their headlines (e.g. "...Local Girl Survives Avalanche of History Papers").

Jubilee: Sharing the Wealth

In biblical times, wealth and power were directly related to the ownership of land. By calling for the *redistribution of wealth*, the vision of Jubilee called for land reform. Today we define wealth in broader terms. While many of us live in a world of plenty, many more live in poverty. The wealthiest fifth of the world's people are more than 60 times wealthier than the poorest fifth. There are 440 billionaires in the world, and each of them is wealthier than six million of the world's poorest people combined! The vision of redistribution of wealth is not one of charity but of generosity. Generosity means sharing the best of what we have, not merely distributing the leftovers, or what we no longer have use for.

An Unequal Share

You will need: play money, snacks (e.g. pop, individual bags of chips, mini-size chocolate bars, cookies)

Instructions: Write the price list on newsprint (e.g. pop=$100, chips=$200, chocolate bars=$200, cookies=$75). Place the amounts (in parentheses) of play money in envelopes marked Latin America ($50), North America ($500), Europe ($250), Asia ($100). Set out snacks and price list. Explain that group members will need to buy their snacks with the play money you give them. Distribute envelopes randomly. Allow group members to "buy" their snacks. Listen and observe their reactions. Talk about the experience and share observations (e.g. people exclaiming "That's not fair!" or someone choosing to share money/food).

Discuss:

- What did it feel like to get less/more money than others?

- How did it feel to accept help from others to pay for your snack?

- Was anyone willing to share their food but not their money? Why was that?

- Which countries got the most money? the least? Why do you think that is?

- What do you think about the food left over?

- How does this exercise relate to the situation in the world today?

Did you know?

A woman named Lizzie Magie invented the game of Monopoly. She was a Quaker. She realized that once someone owned a lot of property it was possible to make lots of money and buy lots more property. On the other hand, people without property often got poorer and poorer. Magie made up the game to show how unfair this is, and called her game "the landlord's game" (US Patent #748,626). Many of her Quaker friends began playing it. They made their own boards and used buttons for markers, added Community Chest, Chance, the $200 for passing Go, and started calling the game Monopoly.

A group of teachers in Philadelphia decided to give the properties names of streets in their town. It was from one of these people that Charles Darrow learned the game. He told the Parker Brothers company that he had invented the game, and sold it to them. Parker Brothers later discovered that this wasn't true, but they covered up the real story.

Many years later there was a court case because Parker Brothers sued a man named Ralph Anspach who started selling a game called "Anti-Monopoly." The real monopoly story came out. The United States Supreme Court ruled that Parker Brothers doesn't have a monopoly on the name Monopoly. The game was in the "public domain" – which means that so many people were part of creating it that it really belongs to everyone.

Adapted from an article by Alyson Huntly, *Worldwind Magazine*, 1995.

Alternative Monopoly

Monopoly is often viewed as a game where people invest their money wisely, and where they get money because they have spent money. People who do not buy property (houses or hotels) often lose the game, and people who risk more money early in the game often end up getting more and more money. This game clearly demonstrates how in the world, the rich get richer and how the poor often get poorer. The game ends when someone loses all of their money.

You will need: the game of Monopoly

Instructions: Copy the **Alternative Monopoly** pages 117–118 and cut cards apart. Divide these into two piles. Place cards face down on the game board where the Community Chest and Chance cards normally go. Follow the rest of the rules as usual (e.g. begin the game with each player receiving $1500).

Play one game using the cards for the lesser-developed country and another game as a more developed country.

Discuss:

- What aspects of monopoly are true to real life?
- Do the rich really get richer and the poor get poorer?
- In the game of Monopoly, everyone starts off with the same amount of money. Is that true in real life? How might this change things, if people do not start on the same foot financially?
- What kind of changes were there between the traditional Monopoly game and the addition of the new community cards? Which game version, the traditional or the other one, is more realistic?

Who Wants to Be a Millionaire?

Discuss the popularity of game shows/lotteries. Why do you think they attract so many people? What would you do with a million dollars? Invite everyone to share their ideas. Then share the following information: In your lifetime, in today's dollars, you will earn on average one million dollars more than you will need for basic necessities. Realistically, how do you think you will spend your million?

Look up some passages about Jesus' teachings on the subject of wealth. Divide into small groups and give each a passage: Matthew 6:19, 24; Matthew 22:15–22; Mark 4:18–19; Luke 6:35; Luke 12:22–23; Luke 14:12–14; Luke 16:13. What do these passages say about wealth? How do you think these teachings apply to you?

How the Church Spends Its Money

Ask the youth what they think the church needs money for and what they think happens to church offerings. Look at the church's annual budget together. Note the amount that is spent on children and youth programs, mission and outreach, and to pay those who work for the church. Many young people may not be aware of how the church supports its youth ministry. This may be in the form of a salary to employ a youth leader, or as an annual budget for supplies and books. Youth groups may be recipients of money earmarked by the church for youth programs, but how do they contribute to these funds? Talk about ways your group might contribute to the overall church revenue (e.g. personal or family offering, plan a special fundraiser). You might decide to donate 10% of all money you raise through youth group fundraisers back to general church funds.

Fair Trade "Alternatives Fair"

November is a popular month for Christmas craft fairs. Why not organize an "Alternatives Fair" to raise awareness and support organizations that sell fairly traded products? Invite local retail stores that sell fairly traded, self-help, or environmentally friendly products to set up a display. Advertise this to congregation members and in the community as an opportunity for people to shop for "Christmas gifts that give twice." Send a press release to local media that might cover the event or offer free advertising. See **Additional Resources** for website addresses of some organizations you might contact.

> **Additional resources**
> Websites of Fair Trade Organizations
> http://www.transfairusa.org
> http://www.serrv.org Find out how your church or non-profit group can sponsor a sale.
> http://www.villages.ca Ten Thousand Villages, a non-profit program of the Mennonite Central Committee, that sells fairly traded goods.

Closing Worship

Provide current newspapers and news magazines. Invite everyone to take a few minutes to find one image of something they are concerned about and to create a one-sentence description of that concern. Sing Kum Ba Yah. (Remind the youth that this means "Come by here" and that it is a prayer asking for Jesus to be present.) Sing the verse "Someone's praying, Lord" once. Say: "God, hear our prayer for…" and invite a youth to place their image on the worship table and speak their prayer aloud. Then sing the verse again, inviting another person to add their prayer, and so on until everyone has placed their image on the worship table.

A Celebration of the Feast of All Saints

Group Check-in

Have group members say their name and three things they know about their name (e.g. if they are named after someone famous or a relative, what their name means in another language, why their parents chose that name).

What's in a name?

Names are chosen carefully; our name is part of our identity. Look up the origin of group members' names in a baby names book and share this. Brainstorm names of saints that group members know (e.g. Nicholas, Patrick, Christopher, Columba). What do we know about these saints? What do their names mean? What is a saint?

Name Bingo

This game works best with groups of five or more. It's a great way to help group members learn each other's name.

Instructions: Copy the **Bingo Card** on page 114. Give a card to each group member. Ask everyone to introduce themselves, using their first name only. Group members write each person's name down in a separate square of their bingo card. Repeat names if the group is small or include names of saints to completely fill the squares of the card. Write names randomly so that everyone's card is different. Give each person 25 pennies, stickers, or a bingo dabber. Write the names of group members (and saints) on slips of paper and place these in a container. Mix them up and draw one, reading the name aloud. Players may mark that square on their bingo card. (If the name appears twice mark only one square.) Continue drawing names until someone has "Bingo" (i.e. a completed line running across, diagonally, or horizontally on their bingo card). Award prizes.

Name Crosswords

You will need: 1 in. (2.5cm) squares of colored construction paper, felt pens
Have each person write each letter of their name on separate squares of paper. Play a Scrabble-type game with the letters, working cooperatively. How many different ways can the letters go together to create new words? If you want to make it more challenging, use last names and first names. This could be mounted on poster board and kept on the wall of the room, adding new names as new people join the group.

What Is a Saint?

The story goes that one day a minister asked the children, "What are saints?" A bright young child pointed to the colored stained glass windows that depicted many of the saints and replied, "Saints are people that light shines through." Saints are indeed ones through whom God's light shines. So that includes you and me, too. We are all part of the Communion of Saints.

The official process the church uses to name a saint, called *canonization*, has only been used since the tenth century. For hundreds of years, starting with the first martyrs of the early church, saints were chosen by public acclaim. In 1983, Pope John Paul II made sweeping changes in the canonization procedure. The process begins after the death of a person whom people regard as holy. The person's life and writings are examined and then a panel of theologians at the Vatican evaluates them. After approval by the panel and cardinals of the Congregation for the Causes of Saints, the pope proclaims the person "venerable." The next step, *beatification*, requires evidence of one miracle (except in the case of martyrs). The miracle must take place after the person's death and as a result of a specific petition to them. Only after one more miracle will the pope canonize the saint (this includes martyrs as well).

The title of "saint" tells us that the person lived a holy life, is in heaven, and is to be honored by the universal church. Canonization does not make a person a saint; it recognizes what God has already done. Canonization takes a long time and a lot of effort. So while every person who is canonized is a saint, not every holy person has been canonized. You have probably known many saints in your life, and you are called by God to be one yourself.

Child and Youth Saints

Read together the stories of young people who made a difference from **Child and Youth Saints** on page 32. How are these people ones whom God's light shines through? What qualities of a saint do they have? What other people would you name as saints? Why?

Icon Posters

You will need: examples of iconography, a Polaroid camera (or ask group members to bring a photograph of themselves, preferably a close-up such as a school picture), paper, pencils, fine-tipped markers, gold/silver gel pens. Look at the examples of icons you've brought. Frequently, we see saints portrayed in paintings with a particular expression  or gesture, in a particular situation or holding or wearing something that symbolizes the work they did or a cause they championed. What can you tell about these saints from these pictures? The light of God's presence in saints is sometimes depicted as light shining through a person's garments and flesh, but especially from their head, in a globe. We too belong to the "Communion of Saints" and we try to live faithfully. Hand out sheets of paper and art materials. Invite youth to create icon posters. Glue photos in the center of the page. If they wish, include a globe or halo in the picture. Invite them to draw symbols around the pictures of things that are important to them and which symbolize their convictions as someone living out the Christian faith.

Personal Coat of Arms

You will need: copies of the **Coat of Arms** pattern on page 34, felt markers, pencils

The term "coat of arms" probably originated in the Middle Ages from the practice of embroidering family emblems on the surcoat, or *tabard*, worn over chain mail. Although a coat of arms had military uses, families, colleges, and cities also designed coats of arms that incorporate symbolic objects and colors. The coats of arms of Jesus' twelve apostles symbolize something significant about their ministry or the way in which each was martyred. Look at examples of coats of arms and talk about each one's symbolism. Invite youth to design their own personal coat of arms depicting some of their personality traits and passions.

Slide Presentation

Create a slide presentation. Take photographs of people in your church community. Use slides in worship as part of a prayer of thanksgiving for the saints in your church (both living and dead). This might be accompanied by a hymn such as *For All the Saints* or *I Sing a Song of the Saints of God.*

Fall Festival

Host a congregational party. Encourage everyone (not just children!) to come dressed as Bible characters or saints. Sing campfire-style songs and offer activities such as face painting, guessing the number of pieces of candy in a jar, bobbing for apples, bean bag toss, cookie decorating, or drawing jack-o'-lantern faces on balloons.

Additional resources

http://saints.catholic.org   Search the Saints Index at the Catholic Online website
http://www.bridgebuilding.com   This website of iconographer Robert J. Lentz includes icons of traditional and modern saints such as St. Francis, Joan of Arc, Martin Luther King Jr., and Gandhi.
http://www.popularbabynames.com   Find the origin and meaning of names

---

Closing Worship

If group members created a personal coat of arms or icon posters, place these around a candle. Stand in a circle to read the litany prayer from page 31.

A Litany of Standing with the Saints

One: We remember, O God, those through whom you have acted – in the world, in the church, and in our own lives. We invoke their names, that they may stand beside us and provide us with the insight of their lives and the encouragement of their prayers:

One: Ryan White, who fought against prejudice and fear of people with AIDS; who encouraged compassion for those infected with HIV, and who died at the age of 17.

ALL: Stand beside us.

One: Anne Frank, whose writings have inspired many to work for peace and an end to racism; who died at the age of 15 in a Nazi concentration camp.

ALL: Stand beside us.

One: Craig Kielburger, whose sense of justice and fairness helped raise awareness about the plight of child workers who are exploited and sold into slavery; whose actions showed the "power of one" to make a difference.

ALL: Stand beside us.

One: Samantha Smith, who dared to write a letter and became an ambassador for peace; who reminded us of God's vision for a peaceful world.

ALL: Stand beside us.

One: Trevor Ferrell, whose compassion continues to inspire people to care for the homeless and those who are less fortunate.

ALL: Stand beside us.

One: Terry Fox, who lost his leg to cancer but did not lose his hope of finding a cure for the disease; who mounted a Marathon of Hope to raise money for cancer research, and who died before he reached his goal.

ALL: Stand beside us.

One: For these and all the saints, past and present, who inspire us and help us to know God better, we give thanks.

ALL: Amen.

A Litany of Remembrance

For those affected by the tragic events of September 11, 2001

God of goodness, we come before you to pray for all people who are preparing for the night. We ask you to watch over all those who are traveling and at work. We ask you especially to be with those whose lives were changed forever by the tragedy of September 11. Those who were on the hijacked flights. Those who were at work in the World Trade Center and the Pentagon. We pray for those mourning the loss of someone they knew. We pray for the depressed, for those forever affected by the devastation they saw. We pray for the victims and also for the perpetrators. Although our human hearts may not forgive, we know your love is greater than ours. We trust in this:

You are awake with those who are awake. You are the sleep of those who are sleeping, and the dying live in you.

Stay with us, because the night is coming, and the day has come to an end.

Stay with us and with all people. Stay with us in the evening of the day, in the evening of our life, in the evening of the world.

Stay with us with your grace and goodness, with your word and sacrament, with your comfort and blessing.

Stay with us, when the night of mourning and fear comes to us, the night of doubt and helplessness, the night of death. Stay with us and with all your children, in time and eternity.

Adapted from the worship book for the Ecumenical Assembly of Graz (23–29 June 1997).
Used with permission of the Council of European Episcopal Conferences
and the Conference of European Churches.

Child and Youth Saints

Trevor Ferrell

At age 11, Trevor saw a TV news clip about the homeless in Philadelphia, the city in which he and his parents lived. The news report talked about the hardships faced by the city's homeless as Christmas approached and the weather got colder. Trevor convinced his father to drive him through the areas where homeless people hung out. At one stop along the way, Trevor jumped out of the car and gave a pillow and a blanket to a man sleeping on the streets. The following night he and his family returned, taking food as well. Soon Trevor had his parents driving him regularly to the city to distribute food and blankets to the homeless. As others heard about what they were doing, they began to receive donations of food and clothing. Out of Trevor's determination and belief that people do make a difference sprung "Trevor's Campaign for the Homeless." An abandoned hotel was donated to the campaign to fulfill Trevor's dream of a home for the homeless. The shelter was named Trevor's Place. More hard work and donations resulted in Trevor's Next Door, the building next to Trevor's Place that offers a residential living center for women and children and provides 24-hour day care, social services, and educational programs. Trevor's father, Frank, says that their family "believes that God has given every human being special gifts, qualities, and talents. Trevor's campaign works to help individuals in need to discover their unique blessings through education, motivation, assistance, and love."

Samantha Smith

When she was just 10 years old, Samantha Smith woke up wondering "if this was going to be the last day of the earth." She had read about the nuclear arms race and was worried that there might be a war between the United States and Russia. Encouraged by her parents, she wrote a letter to Soviet President Yuri Andropov. In her letter she asked the Russian president if he was "going to vote to have a war or not? If you aren't, please tell me how you are going to help to not have a war. God made the world for us to live together in peace and not to fight." Mr. Andropov responded with a long, thoughtful letter in which he invited Samantha and her parents to visit the Soviet Union. Samantha became a symbolic ambassador for peace to Russia. While she was there, she visited the Artek Pioneer Camp where she met and talked with several children her own age. Samantha spent her time swimming, talking, and learning Russian songs and dances. She found that many of her new friends were also concerned about peace. Samantha realized that in many ways the Russian children were not all that different from her and her friends in the United States. Although Samantha and her father died in a plane crash in 1985, her mother Jane founded the Samantha Smith Center in her memory. The main project of the Center is its Youth Summer Camp Exchange with Russian and American kids each attending camp in the other country. The exchange helps to promote international cooperation and understanding. What would Samantha have thought of all this? Her own words provide a hint. "Sometimes I still worry that the next day will be the last day of the Earth," she once said, "but with more people thinking about the problems of the world, I hope that someday soon we will find the way to world peace."

Terry Fox

Terry Fox was diagnosed with bone cancer at the age of 18. His right leg was amputated six inches above the knee and he was fitted with a prosthetic leg. While in hospital, Terry was so moved by the suffering of cancer patients that he decided to run across Canada to raise money for cancer research. His "Marathon of Hope" began in April 1980 at St. John's, Newfoundland. He ran an average of 42 km each day for 143 days. In September, Terry learned that the cancer had spread to his lungs. Just outside of Thunder Bay, Ontario, on September 1, Terry was forced to end his marathon. Ten months later Terry died at the age of 22, on June 28, 1981. Terry's courage and spirit continue today as each year hundreds of thousands of people participate in the Terry Fox Run to raise money for cancer research. To date 21 million dollars has been raised.

Craig Kielburger

When Craig Kielburger was just 12, he read an article on the front page of his local newspaper about a boy from Pakistan named Iqbal Masih who had been sold into bondage at the age of four to work as a carpet weaver. Iqbal was chained to a carpet loom for 14 hours a day and forced to tie tiny knots to make rugs. Craig was touched by the difference between his life and Iqbal's. He gathered information about child labor and brought together friends and classmates to discuss what they could do about this problem and how they could help. Craig helped found Free the Children, an international network of children helping children. It has chapters in more than 20 countries.

Anne Frank

Anne Frank was born in 1929 in Frankfurt, Germany. In 1933, the National Socialist Party, led by Hitler, came to power. Anne's Jewish parents, Edith and Otto, decide to move the family to the Netherlands. Anne was four years old. She grew up, mostly, without a care in Holland. Then, in 1940, when Anne was 11, Germany invaded the Netherlands and the protection that Holland provided came to an end for her family. Their lives were increasingly restricted by the anti-Jewish decrees and in 1942 Holland began to deport Jews to "work camps." Anne's parents decided to hide the family, with the help of their Dutch friends, in the annex of the building that housed Otto's business. During the two years the family lived in hiding, Anne wrote in her diary about their experiences and their fear of being discovered. The letters she wrote in it to her imaginary girlfriend "Kitty" give a personal and moving account of one who lived through the horror of the Holocaust. In August 1944, the people in hiding were indeed discovered. They were arrested and deported. Anne was sent to the Bergen-Belsen concentration camp. She and her sister died of typhoid in the camp in March 1945, just weeks before it was liberated. In 1957, a museum was established on the site where Anne and her family lived in hiding for nearly two years. One of the goals of the Anne Frank House is to fight anti-Semitism and educate about racism.

Ryan White

Ryan White was a typical 13-year-old when it was discovered that he had contracted AIDS through tainted blood products he had been given because he had hemophilia, a hereditary disease that prevents blood from clotting properly. He was then living in Kokomo, Indiana. When Ryan tried to return to school he was told he could not, because people feared they would catch AIDS. So he went to court, fighting not only the angry, fearful school district, but also the whole community. Newspaper headlines followed the many legal battles. Though Ryan won the court case, his own fight had just begun. When a bullet was fired at the White home, the family decided to move to Cicero, Indiana. With great courage, Ryan began to speak out against the misconceptions about the disease and called for people with AIDS to be treated with compassion. Ryan appeared at schools and fundraisers across the country and testified before the President's Commission on AIDS. Ryan spoke to celebrities, educators, and politicians, but most importantly he spoke to other teens about HIV and AIDS. Ryan believed that educating people, especially teenagers, about HIV and AIDS is an important part of preventing the spread of this deadly disease. Ryan died on April 8, 1990. Ryan had fought valiantly for his individual rights and the rights of all people infected with HIV and AIDS. Ryan left a wonderful legacy – a legacy of education and compassion.

Coat of Arms

Instructions: Enlarge on photocopier

Stereotypes and Prejudice

Group Check-in

Choose a flavor of ice cream that describes how you are feeling right now. Take turns explaining your choice to the other group members (e.g. "Right now I am feeling like bubble gum ice cream – sort of bubbly and energetic").

Stereotype Soiree

You will need: safety pins or tape. Write each of following stereotypes and related comments on a separate piece of paper. *Jock* – I'm only interested in sports; *Brain* – I'm only interested in studying and getting good grades; *Goody-Two-Shoes* – I try never to do anything wrong or bad; *Party Animal* – Life is one big rave for this social butterfly; *Snob* – I'm so popular everyone wants to be me, or at least be with me.

Instructions: Ask for five volunteers to wear the signs. Do not show them what their sign says; tape or pin this to the back of their shirt so others can see and read it. Youth should not reveal to each other what is written on the signs. Ask everyone to imagine they are at a party. They should walk around informally and react to the youth with papers on their backs in ways suggested by the signs. The volunteers may also interact with each other. After a few minutes, ask the volunteers to try to decide who they are based on how the others reacted to them.

Discuss:

- *(To the volunteers)* How did the way others talked to you make you feel?
- *(To the others)* How did you decide how to react/what to say to them?
- Have you ever felt stereotyped? How did it feel?
- What can we do individually and as a group to challenge stereotypes?

Have You Seen My Potato?

You will need: a bag of potatoes that are all roughly the same size

Instructions: Pile the potatoes in the center of the circle. Invite each youth to choose one. Give them several minutes to study their potato. Note its distin-

guishing features, how many eyes it has, its color. Now close your eyes and notice its shape, its weight. Ask them to open their eyes and place their potatoes back in the bag. Mix them up and pile them once again in the center of the circle. Invite them to find their potato again. When everyone has found theirs, talk about how they distinguished their potato from the others when they all looked the same. How do we sometimes view people this way? What groups are sometimes considered "all the same"? What is a "stereotype"? What is "prejudice"? Have you ever felt the victim of a stereotype or prejudice? What was it based on (e.g. your age, skin color, gender)?

Gender Stereotypes

You will need: several magazine ads – one specifically advertising a product for men, another for women

If you have a large group, divide into two and give each group a magazine ad. Invite youth to study these magazine ads and discuss them using the following questions.

- Is sex-role stereotyping evident? What are the indications of this?
- How are people dressed?
- Are the men and women doing different things?
- Is the content sexist?
- What is the camera focusing on?
- What are the positions of women/men?
- Is the same message reaching all members of the audience?
- Is sex relevant to the product?

From *B.C.ing Youth: A Publication of the B.C. Conference United Church of Canada Youth Ministry*, Issue 2, 1992. Reprinted by permission.

Sentence Completion

Television informs and entertains. It is a powerful influence in determining the roles of men and women in society. Young people are especially influenced by its portrayal of gender roles. Divide into small groups of two or three. Give each a copy of the following list and allow 5 minutes to brainstorm their responses. Afterward, compare: Was the activity hard to do? Do you think any of the responses betray stereotypes or prejudice?

1) Write down three things that men like to receive for Christmas.
2) Draw two things that women don't do in the home.
3) Make an inventory of the adults you know and their occupations.
4) List ways that people your age refer to their friends (e.g. guys, kids).
5) Make a list of slang words popular with youth (i.e. to describe something that was really fun, or really boring; a person who is popular or not, etc.).

Invisible Walls

Often, prejudice and stereotypes affect individuals and groups by creating "invisible walls" – barriers to education, vocation, health, and experience. Plan a four- or five-week study on topics that are appropriate to your situation and invite guest speakers. Here's what one group did:

- Physical Ability – At the beginning of the meeting each youth was assigned a particular physical disability (e.g. blindness, in a wheelchair, loss of movement in one arm). We carried on the meeting as usual with games and activities to see how the youth coped in an environment set up for people without physical disabilities, then debriefed afterward.

- Gender – We had our Christian education minister as a guest speaker, to talk about the barriers she encountered to becoming ordained because she was a woman and was married.

- Sexual Orientation – We had a member of the congregation as a guest speaker, to talk about the challenges of being a homosexual living in a predominantly heterosexual society and church.

- Economic Status – We had a woman from Employment and Social Services lead us in a simulation called "The Poverty Game" (this is available through the Department of Human Resources). Each youth was given a different economic situation and had to figure out how to make it through the month. We discussed how poverty can be a barrier to education, meaningful work, and health.

- Age – We began by talking about how youth are often discriminated against because of their age (e.g. rule that "only 3 students are allowed in the store at one time") and how this makes us feel. Then we discussed how the elderly face similar barriers (e.g. forced early retirement).

Closing Worship

Stand in a circle. Invite everyone to close their eyes and outstretch their hands, palms facing up, as a symbol of openness to God. Read the closing prayer.

Prayer:
You call us, O God, to do your work.
You want these hands to serve you;
You want these hands to touch your world with love;
You want these hands to build, to hold, to reach out;
You want these hands to be your hands, O God.
We offer them to you. Amen.

Section B: Seasons of Advent & Christmas

Mood and Flavor of these Seasons

The short seasons of Advent and Christmas are combined in this section, but they are two distinct and different seasons.

The Christian Year begins with the Season of Advent on the Sunday nearest St. Andrew's Day (November 30). Unlike the secular year, which always begins on January 1, the Church Year may begin as early as November 27 or as late as December 3. The season consists of the four weeks leading up to Christmas. The observance of Advent originated in France in the fifth century. Modeled on Lent, Advent was established as a 40-day period of preparation for Christmas that began on November 11, the Feast Day of St. Martin of Tours. In the fifth century, the pope adopted the season for the whole church but shortened it to four weeks so as to acknowledge the pre-eminence of Lent as the most important season of preparation (for Easter, the most important festival of the Christian Year).

Advent is a season of preparation with a mood of expectation and hope. The word *advent* means "coming." At this time the church focuses on the coming of Christ into the world 2,000 years ago. We also focus on the present possibilities of Christ's rebirth within each of us and in our community. We look to the future and the coming of God's reign of shalom. As a season of preparation, Advent is also a time when we examine ourselves and confess that our lives and our world are not as God intended. The color for Advent has traditionally been purple, the color of penitence, although many churches have begun to use the color blue – the color of hope and anticipation – to show a difference in mood from Lent. Scripture readings during this season include the prophets' visions of the coming of God's shalom and of the birth of God's "anointed one," or the Messiah. In the New Testament we read about the coming reign of Christ, in all its fullness, at the end of time.

The Season of Christmas is a joyous one, beginning on December 25 (or at sundown on December 24) when we hear about the angels telling the good news to humble shepherds outside Bethlehem. Many churches hold candlelight services on Christmas Eve and Christmas Day. The season lasts 12 days, ending with the Feast of Epiphany on January 6 (also known as a "little Christmas" as Orthodox Christians celebrate Christmas on this day and not on December 25). The colors for the season are white and gold (or yellow).

Special Days

Some special days occur during Advent. World AIDS Day is December 1*. International Human Rights Day is December 10, marking the signing of the International Declaration of Human Rights. Although these are not part of the Christian Year, many churches recognize these in some way. During Advent some churches have a "white gift" service to collect gifts for Christmas hampers or food banks. (See the story of White Gift Sunday on page 41.)

In addition to the special days of Christmas Eve and Christmas Day, the Season of Christmas includes the Feast of Epiphany on January 6. It is the "twelfth day" of Christmas and marks the end of the Christmas season. The feast celebrates the visit of the Magi to the home of Jesus. Of course, the secular year begins in this season with the celebrations of New Year's Eve and New Year's Day.

* In some years this date may fall in the Season after Pentecost.

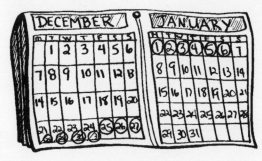

Implications for Youth Ministry

The strong social justice themes of the Season after Pentecost continue in the Season of Advent. As we prepare for Christ's coming, we are aware of the things that are not as they should be and we look at how we can effect change. By Advent most youth group members have developed ties with one another and feelings of trust. They are ready to try new things. They may want to offer leadership beyond the group's own small community.

Most churches have activities they traditionally do during Advent – the "Hanging of the Greens," Advent parties, special services, church school pageants, and outreach projects. The Idea Pages in this section include activities that could be adapted for a congregation-wide event or outreach project that would offer the opportunity for youth participation and leadership. The hard work of group-building throughout the fall yields results when group members work together, combining their talents and interests, to plan a worship service, lead an event, or carry out a project. Afterwards, evaluate together what happened. Did we plan well and follow through on everything? Are there things we would do differently another time? What parts can we affirm and celebrate? Sometimes we forget to evaluate together even though this can be a valuable learning experience for group members. Whether you've completed a project or not, take time as a group to evaluate fall programs. Then plan and dream together about the coming months. Having a "Twelfth Night" Epiphany party is a great way to re-gather after Christmas holidays.

Advent

Group Check-in

Create a feelings forecast. Tape a long strip of banner paper to a wall and hand out markers. Have everyone draw a weather symbol that represents the past or coming week and have them describe this as a weather person might (e.g. "As a high ridge of final exams approaches from the north, expect precipitation").

Longing and Waiting

Divide the youth into two groups. Give each a stack of magazines, a sheet of newsprint, felt marker, and glue. Instruct one team to look for images of things or list things that are instant. For example, fast food, instant banking ads, or time-saving products. Instruct the other team to find or list things that take time. For example, knitting an afghan or taking a walk. After five minutes, share what groups have come up with. Advent is a time to wait, to prepare. How easy or difficult is it to wait for something you really want? What kinds of things are people waiting for at this time of year that are "instant"? What are people waiting for that takes time?

Advent Music

In many churches it is traditional not to sing Christmas carols during Advent. Advent is a season of preparation for Jesus' birth. In a world where information is available to us at the click of a mouse, waiting for anything can seem difficult. It can be a good discipline to wait. Everywhere we go – in the malls, on the radio, in grocery stores – we hear carols. And so in our churches we try to resist the pressure and keep the focus on the advent – the "coming." Look at the words to some traditional Advent hymns such as *O Come, O Come, Emmanuel* and *Hark the Glad Sound! The Saviour Comes*. Look at other songs included in the Advent section of your church's hymnal. What do these songs say about waiting? Who is waiting? What are they waiting for? How are people to wait?

Recycled Advent Wreaths

You will need: aluminum pie plates, aluminum foil, white craft glue/hot glue gun, green spray paint, candles (3 blue/light purple, 1 pink, and 1 white "pillar" candle for each wreath), "junk" (e.g. bottle caps, corks, buttons, plastic bread tabs, leaves cut out of old plastic container lids, six-pack rings)

Instructions: Glue 4 bottle cap "candle holders" to the bottom of an aluminum pie plate at 4 evenly-spaced points around the circle. Scrunch aluminum foil between the candle holders to create a base, leaving space in the center for a white, free-standing Christ candle. Cover the base by gluing on a variety of "junk." Spray paint finished wreaths green. When the paint has dried, extra decorations can be added such as foil ribbons and bows and holly berries made from red buttons or red foil. If the candles are smaller than the candle holders, you will need to glue the candles in place with hot glue or use a small amount of play dough to secure the candles before lighting.

Snow Crèche

Here's a new spin on making a snowman! Make a crèche scene in the snow. Or make a live crèche scene. The crèche scene is thought to have originated with Francis of Assisi. Born the son of a wealthy man in Italy, Francis was renowned for his generosity. He became a monk and took a vow of poverty. One winter night in 1223, on his way to the tiny town of Greccio, Brother Francis saw some shepherds sleeping in a nearby field. Reminded of the shepherds long ago to whom the angel had appeared, Francis decided to create a live nativity scene on a nearby hillside. With a wooden feeding trough, a load of hay, a few animals, and some people in costume, Francis delighted the people of Greccio and helped to remind them of the good news of Christmas. Not long after, Brother Francis died. But the people never forgot the beautiful nativity scene he had made for them. Year after year, they re-created it in the same place. Soon other towns took up the custom as well. In time, the tradition spread all over the world. Crèche scenes with figures of Mary, Joseph, and the others watching over baby Jesus are still familiar sights today.

New Church Year's Eve Party

Reign of Christ Sunday is the last Sunday of the Christian Year. You might plan to celebrate the beginning of a new church year on either Reign of Christ Sunday or the Saturday before Advent 1. Incorporate some traditional New Year's Eve activities such as a countdown, party hats and noisemakers, balloon-drop, and singing *Auld Lang Syne*. Invite group members to pass the peace in place of the usual hugging and "Happy New Year's" to reflect the focus on the beginning of the Season of Advent and a new Church Year.

Storytelling

A timeless Christmas classic is the book *The Best Christmas Pageant Ever*. This is a wonderful story about the Herdmans – Ralph, Imogene, Leroy, Claude, Ollie, and Gladys – six "skinny, stringy-haired kids all alike except for being different sizes and having different black-and-blue places where they had clonked each other." The Herdmans are absolutely the worst kids in the history of the world. They lie and steal; they tease other kids and wreck things. So no one is prepared when the Herdmans storm Sunday school and take over the lead roles in the annual Christmas pageant. The Herdmans had never heard the Christmas story. They didn't know what shepherds were, or what an inn was; they were outraged that Mary had to have her baby in a barn; they called the wise men a bunch of dirty spies and plotted revenge on Herod. And the Herdmans turned a series of disasters into what everyone agrees is the best Christmas pageant ever. Read part of this story over the weeks of Advent or save it for a Christmas sleepover. *The Best Christmas Pageant Ever* has also been made into a movie starring Loretta Swit. Check your local library to borrow a copy.

Additional resources

Simplify and Celebrate: Embracing the Soul of Christmas, Alternatives for Simple Living (Kelowna, BC: Northstone, 1997)
A resource filled with useful ideas and resources to help you reclaim the peace and joy of the season.
The Best Christmas Pageant Ever by Barbara Robinson (New York: HarperCollins, 1972)
The tale of the Herdmans who turned a series of disasters into the best Christmas pageant ever.
Kneeling in Bethlehem by Ann Weems (Louisville: Westminster John Knox, 1987)
A collection of poems that can be used in worship, read aloud, or used by individuals for quiet reflection.

Closing Worship

Ahead of time, ask group members to bring a symbol of someone or a situation that they are concerned about this Christmas (e.g. a friend, the environment, refugees, a family member). The symbol could be a figurine, photograph, toy, newspaper clipping, ornament, etc. For example, the *Star Wars* figure of Jar Jar Binks might represent the "alien" or refugee among us.

Place a nativity scene with the figures of Mary, Joseph, and Jesus in the center of a round tray. Invite group members to add the symbols they've brought, explaining what they symbolize. When the scene has been created, light a candle and share a prayer.

Prayer: We gather together to remember what makes Christmas special. For this time, we put aside our thoughts of gift lists and decorating, baking and shopping. We remember the Christ Child and what his birth means to us and our world.

We remember those Christ came to serve, the hungry, the thirsty, the sick, the imprisoned, the grieving. We remember our family and friends, many of whom we see only during holidays like this. Here and now, we make a commitment to take time during these busy weeks to touch the lives of people as Jesus did in his living and as he continues to do today.

Reprinted from *Simplify and Celebrate*, p. 201.
Used by permission.

Idea Page

Gift Giving

Group Check-in

Have group members trace their hand on a sheet of construction paper and write their name in the center of the handprint. Cut these out. Sit in a circle around a candle. Invite group members to share one gift they bring to the group. As they share, place handprints around the candle.

White Gift Service

Share the story of how White Gift Sunday began. If this is not a tradition in your church, the youth could organize the first ever! You might also choose to dramatize the story for children or the whole congregation. Plan how you will do this. (A script for a dramatized version of this story can be found on pages 26–28 of *Live the Story: Short, Simple Dramas for Church*. See **Additional Resources**.)

The Story of White Gift Sunday

During Advent 1903, an incident occurred in the home of a Methodist minister in Painesville, Ohio, that sparked the White Gift Service into being. The minister's children were arguing over two dolls that they had just received in a gift exchange at Sunday school. One was a beautifully clothed expensive doll, purchased by a well-to-do family. The other was a small doll bought at a 5¢ – $1 store. Jealousy abounded. The gift exchange had not enhanced the spirit of Christmas as intended, but had brought out the worst in the two children. The minister's wife had an idea. She remembered the story of the wise king Kubla Khan, and his people. They each gave the king a gift, but each wrapped the gift in white, so all the gifts looked equal. By doing this the love and devotion of the giver became more important than the gift. So the next year she suggested that the children bring gifts wrapped in white to give to Jesus (Christ the King). Then these gifts could be given to people in need in the community and the true spirit of Christmas would shine through. This started a custom that has been followed by many churches every year since that time.

Preparing the Way

Read Luke 3:1–6. Have two members of the group act out the drama **Prepare!** on page 43, or read the conversation between John the Baptist and Santa Claus with half the group reading the part of John and the others reading the parts of Santa. Talk about ways that people prepare for Christmas. What traditions at home or church are meaningful for you? How do these help you prepare for Jesus' coming in the way that John describes?

Making Gifts

Reclaim the joy of making a gift for someone else with your own hands. Invite someone who enjoys doing arts and crafts to help group members make something to give away – a live wreath, ornaments, candles, soap, a table centerpiece.

Mitten Tree

Sponsor a Mitten Tree (or Sock Tree). Invite the congregation to bring mittens (socks) to hang on a bare branch tree in the church. Or you might string a long "clothesline" in a prominent spot in the sanctuary and encourage people to bring mittens, scarves, hats, jackets, and blankets or sleeping bags to hang on the line. Donate these items to a local out-of-the-cold program, downtown mission, or homeless shelter.

Bulletin Board

Create a bulletin board display to encourage people to celebrate in ways that reflect their values of concern for the environment and for others. Cover the board with paper or fabric. Cut a large Christmas tree from green paper. Trace simple ornament shapes (e.g. stars, balls, bells) on paper and cut out. Write ideas for caring for the environment, sharing with others, and promoting peace and justice on the shapes, and decorate the tree.

Examples

- Buy gifts that "give twice" by supporting local and global fair trade and charitable organizations (e.g. UNICEF, Amnesty International, SERRV, Wildlife Federation, SPCA).
- Wrap gifts in recycled papers such as newspapers, old maps or posters, picture pages from last year's calendar.
- When buying groceries, add a few non-perishable goods to your shopping cart to donate to your local food bank.
- Wrap gifts in fabric or paper bags that can be used again and again.
- Instead of lights, decorate outdoor trees with things the birds and squirrels can enjoy: popcorn and cranberry strings or pine cones covered with peanut butter/cornmeal mixture (plain peanut butter can cause birds to choke).

The Cost of Giving

We often think of gifts as something that cost a lot, a gift we give at birthdays or Christmas. Gifts don't always have to cost money, or cost a lot. What other gifts can we give? (i.e. our time, share a talent we have). Give each of the youth $1 and invite them to use it in some way to gift another person during the week. This may require some imagination!

The following week, talk about what they did with the money and how they were able to give a gift to someone else with it. For example, they might have used a pay phone to call a sick friend with a homework assignment, bought a cup of coffee for someone, plugged an expired parking meter.

Additional resources

The Mitten Tree by Candace Christiansen (Golden, CO: Fulcrum Kids, 1997)
A wonderful parable about the magic of giving to others.
The Stone: A Persian Legend of the Magi by Dianne Hofmeyr and Jude Daly (London: Francis Lincoln Limited, 1998)
When the Magi present their gifts, the child gives them in return a small sealed box and a wonderful surprise.
The Fourth Wise Man by Susan Summers (New York: Dial Books, 1998)
Based on the story by Henry Van Dyke, this is a magical story of one man's lifelong search for the Christ Child.
Live the Story: Short Simple Plays for Churches (Kelowna, BC: Wood Lake Books, 1997)
Plays for Thanksgiving, Advent, Christmas, Lent and Easter including dramatic monologues, Christmas plays, and plays for worship.

Closing Worship

Gather around a candle. Read together the responsive reading.

Leader: It was cold, and Mary and Joseph were fearful.

ALL: But that did not stop the birth.

Leader: They were poor and had no room waiting for them.

ALL: But that did not stop the birth.

Leader: They were uncertain what God wanted from them.

ALL: But that did not stop the birth.

Leader: And today we are still sometimes cold and fearful, certainly poor in so many ways, and unclear about what God wants of us.

ALL: But that need not stop the birth. Be born in us today. Amen.

Prepare! By Ralph Middlecamp

John enters singing "Prepare Ye" from the rock opera *Godspell*. If you are not able to use this music you might substitute Verse 1 of "Joy to the World!" Santa enters a little later than John singing "Here Comes Santa Claus."

(John and Santa meet at Center Stage. John looks with surprise at Santa, then addresses the congregation.)

John People of God! I, John, call you to prepare the way, for the Lord is coming into your lives.

Santa And my name is Santa Claus. I just dropped in to help John out.

John You are going to help me?

Santa Sure! I heard that you and these people are preparing for Christmas and, since Christmas is my business, I thought I might be able to give you a hand. *(Santa drops the bag from his shoulder and reaches in.)* Now I have a stack of Christmas catalogs to be handed out. This should help us get started. I'll begin over here. *(He starts toward the pew.)*

John Wait! What on earth do you think you're doing? I have come to tell these people to prepare for the coming –

Santa Relax, J.B. All these people probably know already that they have to prepare, and they know they don't have much time. As a matter of fact, all the preparations are driving some of them crazy. So let's try to help them. *(He turns back to the people, while pulling items out of his pack.)* Now let's see, friends... here's a list of places selling Christmas trees... These are some sample cards for you to look at from UNICEF... Look at these wreaths that the Scouts are selling... and here are instructions on mailing packages from the Post Office –

John Stop! Please stop! All of this is nonsense! You have not even mentioned Jesus the Savior. It's his coming that we're preparing for. That's why we have gathered to celebrate.

Santa Savior? Oh, right, the crib scene. I was just getting to that. *(He digs into his pack and pulls out a small plastic crèche.)* I do have some dandies. This figure should adorn each of your homes during this season. Just the thing to keep Christ in Christmas. Keep passing those gift books around. Hey John, how about this, a copy of "The Real Christmas Story" with 58 color illustrations.

John Santa, I still don't think you understand. We don't prepare for Christ by showing "baby pictures" but by making room in our hearts and in our lives for him.

Santa Well, my bag is almost empty. I must be missing something.

John All of your gifts are good ideas; they remind us of God's great gift to us, Jesus Christ. The decorations are nice too, but how are you preparing yourself? If God loved the world so much and became a part of it in the birth of Jesus, the least we can do is to welcome Christ with open hearts.

Santa I think we should all try to do that.

John I hope so. The reason I come every year at this time is not to remind you to celebrate an event that has already happened. I ask you to prepare, because you meet Christ in your lives every day. *(John exits singing "Prepare Ye" again.)*

Santa *(Beginning to repack his bag.)* I am afraid that my bag was a little too full of tradition and a little short on love. Sure, we are all going to prepare for Christmas in our own special ways. But let's not become so involved in these preparations that we forget to celebrate God's great gift to us of Jesus Christ. John is right. You may meet Christ this Christmas, so give generously to everyone the best of all gifts, the gift of love. *(Santa exits, also singing "Prepare Ye.")*

Idea Page

AIDS Awareness

Group Check-in

Provide paper and pens. Invite group members to choose an emoticon to express how they are feeling. Emoticons, or emotional icons, are symbols used by Internet users to convey a range of emotions. The more well-known symbols (read sideways) include **:-)** (smiling), **:-D** (laughing), **:-o** (shock), **:-(** (frowning), and **;-)** (winking).

Who's In and Who's Out

You will need: blue and green paper cut into strips
Instructions: Write three or four descriptions like the examples below on separate slips of blue paper. Be careful to choose things that people are not normally ostracized for. For a large group, repeat instructions so that more than one person has the same instruction. On slips of green paper write the instruction: "In everything do to others as you would have them do to you; for this is the law and the teachings of the prophets" (Matt. 7:12).

Divide the group in half. Give one half of the group blue slips of paper, and the other half green slips. Form two circles, with one inside the other. All those with green instructions should form the outside circle. Those with blue instructions form the inside circle, so that for every person in the inside circle there is a corresponding person in the outer circle. Have them stand facing each other. While following the instructions written on their papers they should follow some simple direction such as to greet one another and describe what they did on the weekend. Give them one minute to do this and then have everyone on the outside of the circle move one space to their left. Give another simple direction and so on. Halt the exercise after a few minutes.

Examples of instructions

You must not touch or associate with anyone who
...is wearing running shoes
...has a name that begins with a vowel (a, i, e, o, u, y)
...has blue eyes
...has eaten ground beef in the last three days

Begin the debriefing by having everyone share what the instruction they had been given was. Allow time to explore group members' feelings. How did people treat each other? How did that make you feel? How did it feel to follow the instruction you'd been given? Did anyone ignore their instruction, or feel tempted to but didn't? Why or why not?

Why do you think the people with blue instructions were in the inside circle and those with green instructions on the outside – what might this represent? These were silly instructions; what real-life situations might they represent? What are some reasons people might feel excluded or outcast?

Disease in Biblical Times

In Jesus' time, there were many laws that Jewish people had to follow in order to remain "ritually clean." If you were "unclean" you were not able to enter a place of worship; sometimes you had to live away from other people, such as people with leprosy did. If a person touched an unclean person, they also became unclean until they could do something that would make them clean again, such as offering a sacrifice or observing some ritual. There are 613 of these purity laws in the Torah, in fact, that are also recorded in our Bible. (You might have the youth look through the Book of Leviticus and read some of the headings to get a sense of these laws. Some, like laws about mildew and food, may seem as silly or trivial as the instructions they were given in the game, yet these were important rules for Jewish people.) What laws or social conventions do we have today that might be similar?

Look at the stories from **Accepted or Outcast?** on page 48. Then reflect on the following questions:

• What rules or social conventions about AIDS are suggested in these stories?

• How are people who have HIV/AIDS treated like people who were considered unclean in Jesus' time?

• Who in these stories felt like an outcast? Why?

• How do you think the church should or could respond to these situations?

The Crisis of AIDS

Since the first clinical evidence of AIDS was reported two decades ago, HIV/AIDS has spread to every corner of the world. Still rapidly growing, the epidemic is reversing development gains, robbing millions of their lives, widening the gap between rich and poor, and undermining social and economic security.

• An estimated 36.1 million people are living with HIV. In 2000, about 5.3 million people around the world became infected, 600,000 of them children.

• Sub-Saharan Africa is by far the worst affected region in the world. An estimated 25.3 million Africans were living with HIV at the end of 2000. By that time, a further 17 million had already died of AIDS.

• Some 12.1 million children have lost their mother or both parents to the epidemic.

• By the end of 2000, an estimated 1.1 million children under 15 were living with HIV, largely due to mother-to-child transmission.

Awareness Raising

Offer these candles to members of your congregation on the Sunday before December (World AIDS Day). Ask for donations to support the work of a local AIDS resource center or project.

You will need: inexpensive tapers, red ribbon, 4 x 6 in. (10 x 15 cm) squares of paper, a hole-punch

Instructions: Copy the phrase "This December 1, light one candle for hope" on squares of paper. Using the ribbon, tie these around the candle. Encourage people to light these candles as part of their personal prayers on December 1 for those affected by the AIDS epidemic.

Additional resources

http://www.unaids.org The website of The Joint United Nations Program on HIV/AIDS

Closing Worship

Invite group members to place both feet flat on the floor. Let your hands rest in your lap. Close your eyes. Gently cover your ears with your hands and take four or five deep breaths in and out. Notice the sound of your breath, your heartbeat. *(When everyone has uncovered their ears...)* As you uncover your ears, notice that sounds have become sharper. With your eyes closed, listen to the sounds around you. What sounds do you hear in this room? What sounds do you hear just outside the room, in the hallway? Note what this moment sounds like. When you are ready, open your eyes.

Read the **Litany for Listening** from page 47 together.

A Litany for Listening

One: Holy God, into this world you have sent prophets and visionaries to show us the way, but we have not listened. God, in your mercy...

ALL: Forgive us.

One: You called John the Baptist and sent him into the desert. "Prepare the way of the Lord," he told the people. "Turn from your ways and be baptized into new life!" But many people did not listen. They ignored the message because it was too hard for them to hear, or because they thought they were already living the way you wanted them to. You saw the hardness of their hearts and still your heart was not hardened against them. Holy God, into this world you have sent your prophets and visionaries to show us the way, but we have not listened. God, in your mercy...

ALL: Forgive us.

One: You called Mary, a peasant, a teenage girl, and through her Jesus was born. "My heart praises the Lord; my soul is glad because of God my Savior," Mary said. God has brought down mighty kings from their thrones, and lifted up the lowly. Into this world Jesus brought your good news, but he too was rejected. Holy God, into this world you have sent prophets and visionaries to show us the way, but we have not listened. God, in your mercy...

ALL: Forgive us.

One: Throughout history you have called men, women, and children to speak your word; you have called to Oskar Schindler, Dietrich Bonhoeffer, and to those who resisted the Jewish Holocaust; to Martin Luther King Jr., Rosa Parks, Nelson Mandela, Desmond Tutu, Mahatma Gandhi, and to those who have fought against racism; to Dom Helder Camara, Oscar Romero, and to those who have been voices for the poor in Latin America; to Ryan White, Jon Gates, Lady Diana, and to those who have helped us find compassion amidst the fear of AIDS; to Dorothy Day, Jean Vanier, Mother Teresa, and to all those who have not let us forget the poor, the homeless, the unloved among us. For the times we have not listened, God, in your mercy...

ALL: Forgive us.

One: Help us to hear the voices of your prophets and visionaries. Give us the grace to live each day aware and alert for the possibilities each moment holds. Help us to be ready for the call to be your people for a new day. Amen.

Visit to an AIDS Hospice

After her death in 1997, people all over the world reflected on the life of Diana, Princess of Wales. In Canada, many remembered her visit in 1991.

While in Toronto, Diana made a visit to Casey House, a 12-bed AIDS hospice. At the time, Diana had just begun to express concern in public for issues such as AIDS. Her visit to Casey House was surprising to many who thought she might choose a less harrowing setting than a hospice full of very ill people in the later stages of the disease. Despite expert medical advice to the contrary, many people still feared the virus could be transmitted by touching.

Diana's visit to Casey House was planned carefully. The media were to be excluded out of respect for the residents' privacy; however, one resident – quite ill but well enough to be out of bed – volunteered to meet the Princess just inside the front door and be photographed with her. An observer remembers how the man sat nervously in a wheelchair and how he reacted in awe when he first saw Diana. A chair had been placed at a discrete distance from the man. When she entered the room Diana sat down, then hitched the chair closer, and put her hand on his.

"In my view," recalls writer and founder of Casey House, June Callwood, "pictures of Diana nestled close to a man with AIDS gave more information about HIV transmission than a trillion public health brochures."

Diana moved from room to room, meeting residents, taking the time to sit on their beds, hugging them. In the residents' lounge, she met an emaciated Kenneth Roe, a former school principal from a small town who was more distraught that he had embarrassed his family than he was at the thought of dying. Roe was flanked by his daughters, Mary Lou and Nancy.

The direct impact of Diana's visit to Casey House is impossible to assess, Callwood admits. What is not in doubt, however, is what Diana did for the Roe family. The daughters returned to their community to find that the chilling disapproval that had surrounded them due to their father's illness had ended...The biggest transformation was in Kenneth Roe. Diana gave him back his dignity. He had been lethargic and longing for death, but the respect she paid him changed that. He became a man with an appetite and the energy to go for walks. In the short time he had left, he looked whole and at peace.

Quotes from the article "Reaching Out in Toronto"
by June Callwood, *Maclean's*, September 15, 1997

Accepted or Outcast?

How to Watch Your Brother Die

When the call comes, be calm.
Say to your wife, "My brother is dying. I have to
fly to California."
Try not to be shocked that he already looks like
a cadaver.
Say to the young man sitting by your brother's
side,
"I'm his brother."
Try not to be shocked when the young man
says,
"I'm his lover. Thanks for coming."
Listen to the doctor with a steel face on.
Sign the necessary forms.
Tell the doctor you will take care of everything.
Wonder why doctors are so remote.
Watch the lover's eyes as they stare into
your brother's eyes as they stare into space.
Wonder what they see there.
Remember the time he was jealous and
opened your eyebrow with a sharp stick.
Forgive him out loud
even if he can't understand you.
Realize that the scar will be all that's left of him.
Over coffee in the hospital cafeteria
say to the lover, "You're an extremely good-
looking young man."
Hear him say,
"I never thought I was good enough looking to
deserve your brother."
Watch the tears well up in his eyes. Say,
"I'm sorry. I don't know what it means to be
the lover of another man."
Hear him say,
"It's just like a wife, only the commitment is
deeper because the odds against you are so
much greater."
Say nothing, but
take his hand like a brother's.
Drive to Mexico for unproven drugs that might
help him live longer.
Explain what they are to the border guard.
Fill with rage when he informs you,
"You can't bring those across."
Begin to grow loud.
Feel the lover's hand on your arm,
restraining you. See in the guard's eye
how much a man can hate another man.
Say to the lover, "How can you stand it?"
Hear him say, "You get used to it."
Think of one of your children getting used to
another man's hatred.
Call your wife on the telephone. Tell her,
"He hasn't much time.
I'll be home soon." Before you hang up say,

"How could anyone's commitment be deeper
than a husband and wife?" Hear her say,
"Please, I don't want to know all the details."
When he slips into an irrevocable coma
hold his lover in your arms while he sobs,
no longer strong. Wonder how much longer
you will be able to be strong.
Feel how it feels to hold a man in your arms
whose arms are used to holding men.
Offer God anything to bring your brother back.
Know you have nothing God could possibly
want.
Curse God, but do not
abandon Him.
Stare at the face of the funeral director
when he tells you he will not
embalm the body for fear of
contamination. Let him see in your eyes
how much a man can hate another man.
Stand beside the casket covered in flowers,
white flowers. Say,
"Thank you for coming" to each of several
hundred men
who file past in tears, some of them
holding hands. Know that your brother's life
was not what you imagined. Overhear two
mourners say,
"I wonder who'll be next."
Arrange to take an early flight home.
His lover will drive you to the airport.
When your flight is announced say,
awkwardly, "If I can do anything, please
let me know." Do not flinch when he says,
"Forgive yourself for not wanting to know him
after he told you. He did."
Stop and let it soak in. Say,
"He forgave me, or he knew himself?"
"Both," the lover will say, not knowing what else
to do. Hold him like a brother while he
kisses you on the cheek. Think that
you haven't been kissed by a man since
your father died. Think,
"This is no moment not to be strong." Fly
first class and drink scotch. Stroke
your split eyebrow with a finger
and think of your brother alive. Smile
at the memory and think
how your children will feel in your arms,
warm and friendly and without challenge.

– Michael Lassell

Reprinted from *The World In Us: Gay and Lesbian Poetry Enters the 21st Century*
Edited by Michael Lassell and Elena Georgiou
(New York: St. Martins Press, 2000). Used by permission.

A New Year/Twelfth Night Party

Group Check-in

Write some carol or hymn titles on a sheet of newsprint. Invite youth to choose one (or another they know) that describes how their Christmas holiday was. You might even have group members sing titles! Some examples: *Silent Night, What Child Is This?, God Rest Ye Merry Gentlemen, In the Bleak Midwinter, O Holy Night, Deck the Halls, Joy to the World, Home for the Holidays, Frosty the Snowman, Do You Hear What I Hear?, I'm Dreaming of a White Christmas, Jingle Bells.*

Guess These Christmas Carols

Make copies of **Name That Carol** on page 121. In pairs, have group members try to figure out what carols are being illustrated. Share the answers. Award a prize to the pair with the most correct guesses.

Answers: 1. *Joy to the World* 2. *Silver Bells* 3. *Silent Night* 4. *Deck the Halls* 5. *(I'm Dreaming of a) White Christmas* 6. *O Little Town of Bethlehem* 7. *O Christmas Tree* 8. *O Holy Night* 9. *The Twelve Days of Christmas* 10. *It Came Upon a Midnight Clear* 11. *Frosty the Snowman* 12. *Go Tell It on the Mountain* 13. *The First Noel* 14. *What Child Is This?*

Personal Collage

You will need: paper, markers, magazines, scissors, glue, pastels, paints, brushes

Create personal collages to reflect on the year that has passed, both the good and bad. Provide a variety of art media for youth to work with. Use the completed collages in a brief worship service. Invite participants to add theirs to a Wall of Memories at the beginning of worship; take these down as part of the closing as you read a scripture passage such as Isaiah 43:19.

Bonfire of the Bad Pages

If you have a suitable spot to do this, plan a bonfire. Invite the youth to write two letters, one describing something they want to remember, are proud of, or would like to do again from the past year, the other one describing something that went wrong, or something they are holding on to (e.g. a grudge against someone). The second letters are burned (unread) in a "bonfire of the bad pages in our lives" to celebrate the opportunity to begin again with a new year, or erase a debt that another owes to you.

Progressive Board Games

Use this idea and others on this page to create a program for a congregational or "all youth" New Year's Eve Party.

Instructions: Invite youth to bring their favorite board and card games that can be played by 4–6 players. Games that can be played in under 20 minutes work best (e.g. Jenga, crokinole, Uno, Twister, trivia games). Set up each game at a table with chairs for four players. Players at a table play that game for 15–20 minutes. Then call for them to find another game. Players should mix up so that they are not playing with the same people.

New Year Crackers

Use your imagination to fill these festive crackers. Examples: dollar-store prizes, bookmarks, slips of paper with appropriate scripture passages.

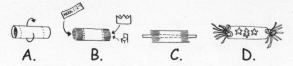

A.   B.   C.   D.

You will need: toilet paper tubes, tissue paper, curling ribbon, stickers, trims, tissue paper (for hats), small prizes, and party snaps (chemically-treated paper that "pops" when it is pulled apart)

Instructions:
Cut tissue paper into 6 in. x 10 in. (15 cm x 25 cm) squares. Use two layers of contrasting colors for a different look. Wrap tissue around the paper tubes and attach with tape or glue along the edge (A). Cut overlapping tissue into a fringe. Stuff inside the tube: prizes, scripture passages, tissue paper hats (B). Place snap inside tube so that it sticks out both ends (C). Tie curling ribbon around each end of tube, gathering up paper to close ends. Decorate the outside with stickers & trims (D).

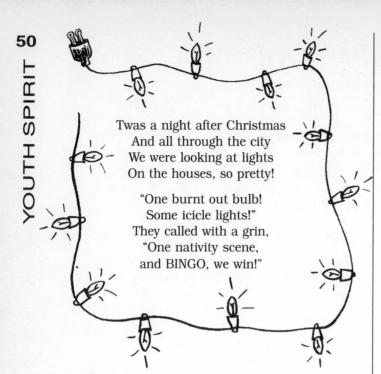

Twas a night after Christmas
And all through the city
We were looking at lights
On the houses, so pretty!

"One burnt out bulb!
Some icicle lights!"
They called with a grin,
"One nativity scene,
and BINGO, we win!"

Christmas Light Bingo

Teams play this fun game of blackout bingo on foot or in cars. Plan to return to the church or a group member's home for hot chocolate afterward.

Instructions: Copy the blank **Bingo Card** on page 114. Write descriptive phrases in the squares such as "Saw an outdoor nativity scene," "Electronic billboard with a Christmas greeting " or "Icicle lights on a house" or "Christmas tree in city park." Make photocopies of the filled-in card. Give each team a bingo card and dabbers or stickers.

Additional resources

The Story of the Other Wiseman by Henry Van Dyke
This timeless Christmas classic is available as a book and has also been made into a movie.
The Fourth Wise Man retold by Susan Summers (New York: Dial Books, 1998)
Based on the story by Henry Van Dyke and beautifully illustrated, this is a magical story of one man's lifelong search for the Christ Child. (The story of the Fourth Wise Man is also retold on p. 83 of *Youth Spirit*, Volume 1.)
These Twelve Days: A Family Guide to After-Christmas Celebrations by James Kasperson and Marina D. Lachecki (OH: United Church Press, 1999)
This seasonal resource is filled with heart-warming stories and traditions to celebrate this holy season.

Closing Worship

Give youth a piece of tape and a paper star shape (see pattern below) and invite them to write their name on it. Create a star garland by taping your star to the next person's, and so on, until they are all attached. Place this around a candle. Light the Christ candle.

Place a crèche scene in the center of your worship table. Add the figures of the Magi. Read *The Story of the Other Wiseman* (see **Additional Resources**). Give youth a glow-in-the-dark star to take home with them as a reminder that they are called to be light in a darkened world.

Prayer: Everlasting God, you guide us to the place where Jesus was born with many signs: dreams, stars, angels. But our world today pulls us in other directions, with neon, Nintendo, and the 'Net. We are tempted with miracles of technology we can hold in our hands, and we are numbed – to the needs of those who so desperately need a sign that somebody, anybody, cares. Forgive our weakness and conspicuous consumption.

You guide us to Jesus so that we might learn your Way and in turn show others. Open our eyes to your signs once again. Give us the desire to see the needs of others and to work to meet them. As you gave your only Son, may we give of our lives and our means, so that others no longer want for even the most basic necessities and can see in us only Jesus as we seek to meet those needs. Make us rays of your light in our darkened world. Amen.

Reprinted from *Simplify and Celebrate*, p. 200.
Used by permission.

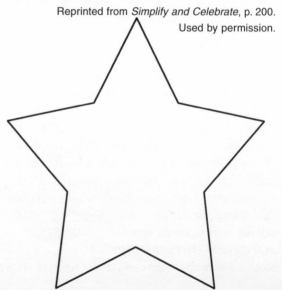

Section C: Season after Epiphany

Mood and Flavor of the Season

The Feast of the Epiphany on January 6 marks the end of the Christmas season. It is the transition to the Epiphany season, also known as the Sundays or Season after Epiphany. There may be as few as four or as many as nine Sundays in this season, depending on the date of Easter and the beginning of Lent. The first Sunday after Epiphany is the Baptism of Our Lord. The season ends with Shrove Tuesday.

The word *epiphany* means "showing forth" or "manifestation." During this season, we see God's glory and purpose "made manifest" through the life and teachings of Jesus. The mood is one of proclamation and growth. The liturgical color for the first Sunday (the Baptism of Our Lord) and for the last Sunday (Transfiguration) is white, symbolizing days of special significance. Otherwise the color of this season is green, symbolizing growth.

During the Season after Epiphany, the gospel readings focus on the call of the disciples, and on the teaching and healing ministry of Jesus. Traditionally, this is a time when the church focuses on its "call" and mission in the world. With his baptism, Jesus began to take specific action in response to God's call. God also summons us, both as individuals and as a people. God's call to us is not something we hear with our ear, but something we feel with our hearts. The lectionary passages for the last Sunday of the Season after Epiphany (Transfiguration) describe a mystical event experienced by Jesus and his followers. These readings provide a unique opportunity for youth to explore their own "awesome" experiences of God.

Special Days

The special days in this season reflect the themes of "call" and mission. January 15 marks the anniversary of the birth of civil rights' activist Martin Luther King, Jr. February marks Black History Month. Many churches observe the Week of Prayer for Christian Unity in late January. The traditional date for the Week of Prayer for Christian Unity is January 18–25. Those dates were proposed in 1908 by Paul Watson to cover the days between the feast of St. Peter and the feast of St. Paul, and have therefore a symbolic meaning. This ecumenical initiative promotes unity between Christian churches that are often divided by historical, theological, and cultural differences. The word "ecumenical" is derived from the Greek term *oikoumene*, which may be translated as "the whole inhabited world." It is in seeing all the world's people as made in God's image that we are called to protect the welfare of every one. February 14 is the feast day of St. Valentine, who was imprisoned and put to death for being a Christian.

Just prior to Ash Wednesday, Canadian churches focus on global concerns and mission projects through the program of Ten Days for Global Justice. During this season, check with your church to learn about your denomination's mission education programs.

The Season after Epiphany ends with Shrove Tuesday. The word *shrove* comes from the verb "to shrive," meaning to confess and receive absolution (God's forgiveness). Shrove Tuesday precedes Ash Wednesday (the first day of the Season of Lent). Early Christians prepared for fasting or eating simple food in Lent by using up the last of foods like eggs, sugar, and milk. This began the tradition of eating pancakes for Shrove Tuesday dinner (a simple way to use up the eggs, milk, and sugar in the house). Today we often refer to this day as "Pancake Tuesday." Some churches combine the feasting with an Ash Wednesday celebration after sundown on Tuesday.

In some places around the world, these preparations are part of *Mardi Gras* ("Fat Tuesday") or Carnival – a time when people indulge in parties, costumes, and good food. The word "carnival" comes from the Latin *carnem levare*, meaning "the putting away of meat." Since early Christians would "give up" eating meat and other rich foods during Lent, both Mardi Gras and Carnival were seen as a last chance to celebrate before a period of restraint. The real reason for all the indulgence and revelry is often lost in the modern-day context, but these traditions do originate from early church tradition.

Implications for Youth Ministry

The themes of "call" and discipleship in the Season after Epiphany are important ones for youth. Like Jesus at the time of his baptism, adolescents are sorting out their identities and discerning the paths they will follow. Today's youth test boundaries, sort out values, search for their "real" selves, and struggle with important decisions about the future. For adolescents this can be both liberating and frightening. The Idea Pages in this section include suggestions for looking at how we are shaped by the media and by the culture around us.

Our religious beliefs are an important aspect of our identity, and youth are at an age when questioning is very important in their faith development. This often includes questioning the role of the church and faith in their day-to-day lives. Youth groups need to be supportive and accepting places where youth can ask their questions and talk about newfound insights. According to research done by Reginald Bibby and Donald Posterski in *Teen Trends: A Nation in Motion*, nearly 60% of the surveyed teens indicated they have spiritual needs and 25% said that spirituality is "very important" to them. The Week of Prayer for Christian Unity offers an ideal time to explore what other Christian churches and people of other faiths believe.

Some youth have a very strong sense of God's "call" in their lives, while others have difficulty recognizing they've ever had an experience of God. Some express doubts about God's presence in their lives at all. According to Bibby and Posterski's research, 81% of teens say they believe in the existence of God and 34% believe they have had an experience of God. The Idea Pages in this section also explore the theme of "call" as we look at ways God's call comes through personal experiences, even in unusual ways such as dreams!

After the Christmas rush, this slower season may be ideal for having a sleepover. Youth can experience living in community and reflect on what it meant for Jesus and his disciples. Organize a viewing of a movie about miracles, the supernatural, or about someone like Rosa Parks or Martin Luther King, Jr., who "lived out their faith" through their actions. A good project for young people is hosting a Shrove Tuesday pancake supper to raise money for a retreat or outreach project. (See Labyrinths and Lent on page 81 for ideas you might incorporate into a Shrove Tuesday celebration.)

Dreams

Group Check-in

Give each person a sheet of paper and a marker and invite them to draw a symbol of something that happened during the previous week. Invite group members to share what they have drawn and describe what it symbolizes.

Warned in a Dream

Begin by reading the story of the visit of the Magi from Matthew 2:1–12. The last sentence of verse 12 tells us that the wise men were warned in a dream not to go back to Herod. Have you ever had a dream like this that provided an important insight or that seemed especially meaningful or significant? What did you do as a result of the dream? What do you think is the purpose of dreams?

Analyze a Biblical Dream

There are many stories involving dreams that are recorded in our Bible. Divide the youth into several small groups and give each a scripture passage. Invite groups to read their passage 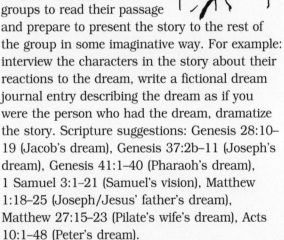 and prepare to present the story to the rest of the group in some imaginative way. For example: interview the characters in the story about their reactions to the dream, write a fictional dream journal entry describing the dream as if you were the person who had the dream, dramatize the story. Scripture suggestions: Genesis 28:10–19 (Jacob's dream), Genesis 37:2b–11 (Joseph's dream), Genesis 41:1–40 (Pharaoh's dream), 1 Samuel 3:1–21 (Samuel's vision), Matthew 1:18–25 (Joseph/Jesus' father's dream), Matthew 27:15–23 (Pilate's wife's dream), Acts 10:1–48 (Peter's dream).

Myths about Dreams

Brainstorm some myths about dreams (e.g. if you dream that you are falling and you don't wake up you will die). Share information from **Dream Myths and Facts** on page 55. What do we know about dreams?

"If this was my dream…"

Do some preparatory work on dreams as a source of guidance and healing. Ask members to write down their dreams before your meeting. If someone has difficulty remembering their dreams, encourage them to ask/pray for a dream they will remember. Also suggest they keep a notebook next to their bed and write down what they remember as soon as they wake up. Next meeting, sit in a circle and have someone share a dream they would like help interpreting. Have other members take turns interpreting the dream as if it were their own. Have them start with the phrase, "in my dream…the monster represents something I'm afraid of … etc." The original dreamer listens and if they get any sudden insights (called "ahas") they share those with the group. It is amazing how much light can be shed on a dream through this simple process. Share information from **Dream Symbols and Meanings** from page 56.

Dream Journals

Create journals to record your dreams!

You will need: inexpensive notebooks or lined notepaper, card stock or coarse paper, tempera paint, coarse salt, stapler

Instructions: To create journal covers, paint card stock covers with watercolors. While still wet, sprinkle coarse salt over the picture and watch the star images emerge! Cut and fold paper covers to the same size as the lined paper or notebook. Staple together.

Additional resources

The Spyglass: A Story of Faith by Richard Paul Evans (New York: Simon & Schuster, 2000)
The story of a king who rules over a darkened kingdom. Crops are planted and then fail, houses are built and then neglected, people are impoverished and dispirited. But when a traveler arrives at the crumbling palace, he shows the monarch his kingdom through the lens of a magic spyglass – a spyglass that shows him his kingdom not as it is, but as it could be.

There is no shortage of books on dream interpretation and meanings in libraries and bookstores. Many of these "dream dictionaries" are less than helpful, offering one-size-fits-all definitions of symbols and dreams. One recommended book is *In Your Dreams: Falling, Flying and Other Dream Themes* by Gayle Delaney, PhD (San Francisco: HarperSanFrancisco, 1997). It provides a dream interview method that will help dreamers discover the distinct meaning of their very personal dreams.

Closing Worship

Invite the youth to make a spyglass using construction paper and tape. Look through the tubes. What do they see? Read the story *The Spyglass* by Richard Paul Evans (see **Additional Resources**). Invite the youth to look through their spyglasses again. If these paper tubes allowed us to see God's kingdom, what would we see? As each person shares their ideas, say in unison: "We have seen the Holy Child. We will go and make these things so."

Prayer:

Epiphanies are glimpses of you, God.
You revealed your love for the world in your son, Jesus,
and your love spread through him, and through his disciples.
It continues to spread today through all who follow Jesus.
Help us, O God, to live our love for you
so that others will glimpse you in what we say and in what we do. Amen.

Dream Myths and Facts

What is (causes) a dream?

Technically speaking, a dream is a period of spontaneous brain activity that usually lasts from about five to 40 minutes and occurs during sleep several times a night, usually at about 90-minute intervals. Have you ever realized you were having a dream while you were dreaming? Dream experts call this a *lucid dream*. Most people have experienced this at some time, often during a nightmare, when the fear of the situation suddenly lifts as you say to yourself, "Wait a minute. This is only a dream."

What is (causes) a nightmare?

A nightmare is a disturbing dream that causes a person to wake up feeling anxious or frightened. The content of the dream is usually easy to recall, often in "vivid detail." Although the plot of the dream may seem silly in the clear light of day, the strong emotions are all too real and may stay with the person for some time. How does a *night terror* differ from a nightmare? A night terror is basically a severe nightmare. They are common in children ages three to five, but can also occur in older children and adults. People who have observed a child having a night terror say that the child wakes up in an extreme state of panic, perhaps screaming out in fear, and appears dazed. Their heart races, they perspire, and they are sometimes difficult to calm down. Yet when they are asked what they were dreaming about, they may not be able to remember.

Myth #1 Some people never dream, or only dream infrequently.

You spend about a third of your life sleeping. And you dream more than a thousand dreams a year – whether you remember your dreams or not. Studies on dream deprivation show that people who are denied their dream time may suffer impaired functioning in a matter of days, possibly becoming disoriented and even depressed. You could go without food and water for several days longer than you could go without dreaming.

Myth #2 Most people's dreams are in black-and-white.

Studies show that dreams take place in color, sometimes as vivid as real life. In fact, in studies in which dreamers were awakened during the dream cycle and asked about color, subjects could remember it about 80% of the time. The reason so many people claim to dream in black-and-white may be that color is not as memorable to them as other aspects of the dream.

Myth #3 Dreams take place in a flash. What may seem like hours is really only seconds.

Sleepers view dreams as though they are watching a film, so they generally take as long to dream as they would to watch or experience. There are several periods of dreaming throughout every night, and these periods get longer and longer as the night progresses. Your final dreaming session may last as long as an hour. The reason many people believe dreams happen in a flash may be because of fleeting images that seem a lot like dreams, which they experience as they fall asleep (hypnagogic dreams) or as they wake up (hypnomonic dreams). These dreamlets are not fully formed dreams.

Myth #4 If you dream that you die, you may actually die.

This idea probably results from the fact that most of us awaken when we dream of crashing in a car, or falling off a cliff, or otherwise endangering ourselves. When you consider that nightmares or scary dreams almost always awaken dreamers, it seems that our tendnecy to rouse ourselves might suggest that we are doing so to save our own lives. But this is not the case. There are many people who have dreamed of dying and awoken the next morning to recount the dream to others.

Myth #5 It is dangerous to awaken a sleepwalker or a person having a nightmare.

Perhaps this misconception stems from experiences people have had of startling a sleeping person into consciousness. The person may have struck out in defense or stumbled and fallen. But it is not psychologically dangerous to wake a sleepwalker. In fact, it is likely more dangerous to let the sleeping person wander around! Whether a person sleepwalks or not, it is best to let them sleep through their nightmare so as to complete the dream. Don't restrain or rouse the person unless necessary. Instead, speak quietly to them, reassuring them that everything is all right. Then let the dreamer return to sleep as soon as possible.

Dream Symbols and Meanings

While no one else can really tell you what a dream means for you, and it is important to attach your own personal meanings to symbols in dreams, there are some archetypes and over-arching themes in dreams that many people share across cultures. We all dream of being chased, of falling, of flying. As humans on one planet, we all share a great number of hopes and fears that are manifested in common themes in dreams.

Remembering Your Dreams

If you have troubling re-membering your dreams, try this! Before going to sleep, as you fall asleep, say to yourself, "I will re-member and record my dreams." Say this several times; try to go to sleep with this thought in your mind. Don't analyze or think too deeply about it, just hold it lightly in your mind. You'll be surprised how it will help with dream recall!

Also:

1. Keep a notepad and pen-cil near your bed. If you wake up from a dream in the middle of the night or in the morning, write it down as soon as possible.

2. When you first wake up, try to lie still and remem-ber your dreams. Some-times it helps to stay in (or return to) the same posi-tion you woke up in.

3. Before going to sleep, jot down the date and three or four lines about what you did and felt that day. This will help you interpret your dream's meaning.

Being Chased

Being chased in a dream is usually frightening. We may dream we are being chased by a person, an animal, even storms, lightning and thunder. Dreamers almost always awaken before they are caught. Dreams of being chased are often about something we are running away from – a person, situation, or fear. Sometimes the dream signals that we are running away from a part of ourselves we refuse to recog-nize. Being pursued in a dream may be a metaphor for feelings of insecurity, powerlessness, guilt or fear of being caught, or a sense that circumstances are "closing in" on us.

Being Unable to Run

Most people have experienced a dream when their legs feel weighted down – like they are running in quicksand – and they just can't move. This dream is sometimes a variation on a dream of being chased, as people often recognize they are unable to run while trying to flee from a pursuer. This dream is usually frustrating and frightening. Dreams where we are unable to run may in fact be a regular chase dream from which we partially wake but do not gain control of our extremi-ties, since the stimulus to our big motor muscles is turned off while we dream. You might look at the section on "Being Chased" above to help you interpret your dream of not being able to run.

Falling Dreams

Almost everyone has at some time been jolted awake by the alarming sensation of falling from a great height. These dreams frequently occur as our body relaxes and we begin to fall asleep. Usually they don't have much meaning on a psychological level. However, we may have other falling dreams during the night that involve story lines. We might dream we are falling off a cliff or out of a plane. Our falling dreams can express anxiety about dangerous, sometimes self-destructive behaviors. Or they may express our fear of losing status, of being put down, or of feeling like a failure. Sometimes these dreams express a sense of loss of control, of losing one's grip, and of being helpless.

Flying Dreams

Many people who have experienced a flying dream find this a pleas-ant experience – the thrill of soaring, the pleasure of flying effort-lessly through the air and doing acrobatic stunts, the feeling of being unbelievably free. Some people fly to friends' houses and visit. Some fly far above the earth. People often describe a feeling of peacefulness that accompanies these dreams. These dreams may be symbolic of feelings of competence or success. There is also a school of thought that connects these dreams of flight to out-of-body experiences, as sometimes people are aware of floating above their physical bodies.

Being Unable to Call for Help

The dream of being unable to call for help can be a very important one that many people ignore. In this dream the dreamer is often in a difficult, dangerous, even desperate situation. At the very end the dreamer tries to call for help – the dreamer calls out but can't make his or her voice heard. Or the dreamer frantically dials 9-1-1 but can't get through, or dials the wrong number; either the telephone doesn't work or the operator is uncooperative. Frequently the dream of calling for help has a parallel situation in the dreamer's life, such as a difficult emotional or career situation that they are unable or unwilling to ask for help with.

Teeth Falling Out

Almost everyone has dreamt of their teeth falling out. Sometimes people dream that their teeth are crumbling into their hands or, worse yet, that they can feel the loose teeth like stones in their mouths. Some people believe that losing one's teeth foretells the death of some member of the dreamer's family, or of a loss of possessions. Most modern dream interpreters believe the dream signifies a fear of "looking bad" or of losing face and can be traced to a recent incident in the dreamer's life when they lost face or said or did something they later regretted.

Being Naked in Public

Nearly everyone has had a dream about being naked or only partially dressed in public and feeling embarrassed or ashamed. Dreamers commonly describe their frustration that they find themselves incapable of making an exit, and that the people who see them don't seem to care – they seem indifferent to their nakedness and suffering. These dreams are generally associated with anxiety about feeling overexposed or vulnerable, or with fears of being criticized.

Cars

Car dreams are very common. We may dream about finding a car we thought we had lost or of realizing we own a car we never knew we owned. We may dream about suddenly driving down the road in a very unusual car of a particular year or color. Sometimes our dream cars have mechanical difficulties. The type of car and the condition of the car can be symbolic. We may dream of driving recklessly or being out of control. Or we may dream of not being the driver but the passenger in the car. Sometimes we sit in the front seat, sometimes in the back seat. Sometimes the driver is capable and sometimes the driver is reckless. Carl Jung proposed that a car symbolizes the way a person moves forward in time; cars or other vehicles represent our personal "vehicles" – our bodies. Cars can also symbolize relationships. For example, if a husband and wife are in a car together, the dream might be about their relationship, and the answer to the question "Who was driving this car?" often suggests who is in control of the relationship. Dreams about driving can represent new direction in life and how you are handling it. Are you in the driver's seat? If not, who or what is driving your life? Is the car out of control? What might this be telling you?

Tips for recording dreams

- After you've reflected on the dream and seem to recall as much of it as you can, write down everything you remember. It is better to begin by writing in "rough notes" anything you can remember about the dream itself, even if only fragments. Dream fragments can in fact be quite important!

- Don't worry about putting details in order. In fact, it is often the case that we will start writing down the dream with the first thing we remember (the last part of the dream before waking) and work backwards to the beginning!

- Record small details in the dream, even if they seem insignificant. Record the feelings or sensations you experienced during the dream, and events from your life that come to mind when you think about the dream (even if you're not sure how those events are related to the dream). You might do this in the form of a map: write a central word or feeling on the page, cluster other words, associations, or dream images around it.

More tips for recording dreams

- Reflect on the dream by considering the events of the day before, any question that has concerned you recently, any recent change in your lifestyle. The dream may be in response to any of these. Ask the question: "Does this remind you of anything or anyone in your life? Does this remind you of any part of yourself?"

- Give the dream a title. What was the focus of the dream? Where was the energy of the dream focused? A one or two word title is usually most effective. For example, "Flight" or "Pursuit." You might play with the title once you've decided on it. Do other phrases easily come to mind? Could the word have a double-meaning? For example, you might title a dream about being chased "Pursuit." Phrases that might come to mind might be: trivial pursuit, the pursuit of happiness. Pursuit can have the meaning of being chased, pursued; it also has the double meaning of career/vocation, as in "refinishing my coffee table is my latest pursuit."

Being Lost

The dream of being lost can go from a simple image of wandering and of feeling lost in a forest, city, or field, to a long and involved dream in which you end up lost, disoriented, not knowing how to get home. Often there will be nobody around from whom you can ask assistance. Dreamers usually feel sad and frightened at the end of such dreams. Most psychotherapists see these dreams as having to do with the dreamer's feelings of being lost in an emotional sense or of having no sense of direction or purpose, or of feeling lost in a spiritual sense, or of feeling terribly alone. Sometimes these dreams carry with them clues as to why the dreamer is lost and thus offer the dreamer a chance to make constructive changes.

Death of Someone You Care About

Although these dreams are very common, they often leave people worrying for days that the dream might come true. Most people dream of the death of someone they love without the dream coming to pass. Within the dream the death may be reported verbally, it may be seen in a newspaper, or it may be heard on the radio. Or sometimes the dreamer will dream in vivid detail about an accident or the death itself. While these are not about what is going to happen, they are about what is going on in the dreamer's life at the time. Often the dead person represents a valued part of our personality that may be dead, repressed, or somehow unavailable to us. The sadness we feel in the dream is often related to our awareness, first recognized within the dream state, of a sadness over such a loss. In some dreams we use the death of someone we love to express our fears of abandonment and insecurity.

Examination Dreams

Many people describe having had dreams where they are frantically searching for the right room, about to take an exam for which they are totally unprepared. The test may take the form of a high school test, a doctoral exam, performing lines in a play, or singing a solo. The test may be illegible or on the wrong topic, or perhaps you realize you forgot to study all term. Sometimes the dreamer realizes that they have already passed the test, years ago. An exam can be a metaphor for tests in the dreamer's life, for a sense of being tested or examined, or for being unprepared for something. If you have this dream frequently, it might be important to consider whether or not you are living a life with so many deadlines and demands that you feel you are never fully prepared. Or consider who the test givers are in the dream and who they might represent in your life.

Idea Page

Exploring What Others Believe

Group Check-in

Provide individual portions of play dough or Plasticine. Invite group members to choose a color and mold it into a symbol of the previous week. Invite them to take turns sharing what they have made and what it symbolizes.

Visiting Other Places of Worship

Arrange to take the youth to the places of worship of other faith traditions: a Buddhist temple, Jewish synagogue, Islamic mosque, Sikh temple, etc. Arrange for a tour or to experience a service of prayer or worship if that is appropriate. Other traditions are usually happy to share their faith, and it can be a once in a lifetime opportunity for many youth. Use the experience to spark discussion about beliefs, racism, and diversity. If it is not possible to visit these other places of worship, have youth/people from other faiths as guest speakers.

The Christian Family – Many Members

Plan to attend worship services at several Christian churches in your area over several Sundays. Consult a phone book or newspaper for times of worship. Use the information on pages 63–64 and other resources to prepare an information sheet about each denomination you visit. Note interesting facts about the denomination's history, beliefs, and worship. Afterward, discuss what the youth liked and didn't like and what was different from your church's worship. What do they think about the differences that have divided the Christian church historically?

Beliefs, Doubts, Questions

Beforehand, write one of the following words on the bottom of paper cups: God, Jesus, the Bible, heaven, church, evil. Serve soft drinks and tell the youth to hold on to their cup. When you are ready, have the youth get into teams based on what is written on the bottom of their cups. Give each team a pencil and pen and ask groups to write down one belief they share about the topic and one doubt or question they have about their topic. You might want to place the questions in a box and use these to spark discussion. Draw one and discuss it fully.

Discuss afterward:

- Did the group have different beliefs/disagreements about beliefs?

- How do you view people who have different beliefs than yours?

Denominational Jeopardy

Create a Jeopardy-like game to explore the different practices and beliefs of Christian denominations. Research "answers." (Players come up with the questions. Remember, their responses must begin with "What is" or "Who is.") For 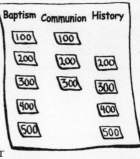 example, if the answer is "In some churches this is used instead of bread in Communion to symbolize Christ's body." The question would be "What is a wafer?" Choose four or five categories and create five questions for each worth 100–500 points. Write the categories horizontally across a sheet of newsprint. Write the amounts on sticky notes; arrange these in columns under the categories. When a team chooses a question remove that amount (sticky note). If the team answers correctly they get the sticky note. Some suggested categories: Baptism, Communion, History, Sacraments.

Week of Prayer for Christian Unity

The Week of Prayer for Christian Unity is normally observed in the week that includes the Feast of the Conversion of St. Paul on January 25. Work with your clergy and leaders in other churches in your community to plan an event to mark the week. You might plan a youth group exchange (like a "pulpit exchange"); your youth group would attend worship at another church while their youth group attends yours. Arrange for both groups to meet afterwards for a social activity and to share experiences. Read a portion of one of Paul's epistles such as 1 Corinthians 12:12–27 which compares the Christian church to a body with many parts. Explain that Paul wrote these letters to churches that he started and that he visited on his many missionary trips, to encourage and teach them. The youth might write a "Dear Friends in Christ" letter to the congregation they visited, offering words of encouragement and thanks for their hospitality.

Closing Worship

Read the children's storybook *The Christmas Menorahs: How a Town Fought Hate* (see **Additional Resources**) or share the story from page 61. Give each member of the group a taper and light these as you read the **Litany Prayer** on page 62 together.

Additional resources

How to Be a Perfect Stranger Vols. 1 & 2, edited by J. Magida (Northstone/SkyLight Paths Publishing, 2000)
This guidebook helps the well-meaning guest to feel comfortable and to participate to the fullest extent possible in others' religious ceremonies. Newly revised North American edition includes Canadian statistics and information.
To the Point: Confronting Youth Issues – Religions (Nashville: Abingdon Press, 1995)
Includes information on world religions such as Judaism, Islam, Buddhism, and Christian denominations including Roman Catholic, Anglican and Episcopal, Quaker, and Pentecostal.
The Christmas Menorahs: How a Town Fought Hate by Janice D.S.W. Cohn and illustrated by Bill Farnsworth (Albert Whitman & Co, 1995)
Based on a true incident that occurred in Billings, Montana this storybook tells how two children, two families – one Jewish, one Christian – and a community resolve to stand together against the shameful actions that have been happening in their town.
http://www.religioustolerance.org This website offers descriptions and information about many faiths from Baha'i to Zoroastrianism.

And They Lit the Menorah

In 1993, there were about 100,000 people living in the town of Billings, Montana. It was a friendly town with several dozen Jewish families; there was one synagogue, Congregation Beth Aaron. Most of the time, the Jewish and non-Jewish people in the community treated one another with respect, although in the past some people who belonged to a hate group had vandalized the synagogue by spray painting graffiti on its doors, and had even desecrated the Jewish cemetery by knocking over the gravestones.

As December approached, decorations began to appear in windows and shops – Christmas wreaths, angels, colored lights. The Schnitzer family, who were Jewish, were preparing for Hanukkah, the Festival of Lights. They placed a stenciled picture of a menorah in the window of their five-year-old son Isaac's bedroom. A menorah is an eight-branch candelabrum. During the eight nights of Hanukkah, Jewish families observe the lighting of the Hanukkah menorah to signify their understanding that our purpose is to illuminate the darkness of this world. That night, someone threw a brick through the window in which the paper menorah hung.

The next day, one of Isaac's non-Jewish friends heard about what had happened. Isaac's friend drew a new menorah for him, so that Isaac could put the drawing of the menorah in his newly fixed bedroom window. When a local Christian minister heard what happened, he asked all the children in Sunday school to make paper-cutout menorahs in their art class and to place them in their windows. A local high school, Central Catholic High, made a sign wishing the Jewish townspeople a "Happy Hanukkah." A local United Methodist Church put a big menorah on its lawn. And a sporting goods store put up a big sign supporting the Schnitzer family. Many other people came to the synagogue that Shabbat to show their support for their Jewish friends and neighbors.

The city's newspaper, *The Billings Gazette*, printed the story about the broken window and the paper-cutout menorahs. To show its support for the Schnitzers, the newspaper also printed a full-page picture of a Hanukkah menorah. More than 10,000 families – of all different faiths – that read the newspaper that day cut the picture of the menorah out, and taped it to their windows. By doing this, they showed the people who had thrown the brick through the Schnitzer's window that everyone deserves to be treated the same, and to live in security, regardless of their race, color, or religious beliefs.

A famous photograph was taken by Fredrick Brenner of members of the Billing's Christian community and leaders of other religious communities standing together each holding a menorah – a profound way of showing love for their neighbors. It was part of an exhibit in New York City in 2001, entitled "Choosing to Participate," that celebrated the power of individual citizens to make a difference and told the stories of ordinary Americans who took a stand in their communities against racism and prejudice.

Litany Prayer

Leader: As we light these candles, help us to remember your call to be beacons of light, to illuminate the darkness of the world. "It is better to light one candle than to curse the darkness."

Leader: Let us seek the forgiveness of God and of each other for the times when we have prejudged people and situations, when we have not questioned stereotypes, not looked past someone's race or skin color or religion to see the person. God, we have sinned against you and each other.

ALL: God, have mercy.

Leader: Let us seek the forgiveness of God and of each other for the times we have not spoken up or acted on behalf of others, because to do so meant risking our own safety, security, or popularity. God, we have sinned against you and each other.

ALL: God, have mercy.

Leader: Let us seek the forgiveness of God and of each other for the hurtful words we have used to categorize people, to label people, to separate "us" from "them." God, we have sinned against you and each other.

ALL: God, have mercy.

Leader: Let us seek the forgiveness of God and of each other for the misunderstanding and intolerance between people of different faiths that has led to hate, to violence, to war. God, we have sinned against you and each other.

ALL: God, have mercy.

Leader: Let us seek the forgiveness of God and of each other for the divisions that have hindered us as a Christian family. God, we have sinned against you and each other.

ALL: God, have mercy.

Leader: Amen.

The Christian Family –
Many Members

Within the Christian Church there are many different branches and denominations. Some of these are quite distinct and unique, while others fall into certain "families" (such as reformed churches, orthodox churches, etc.). On this page you will find the major characteristics of some of the larger denominations. There are probably churches in your community that are affiliated with these groupings and others that are not.)

Eastern Orthodox Church

The Eastern Orthodox Church was formed by a division in the Church around 1050 CE between Christians who believed the Church was unified through its organization and leadership, and others who believed Church unity was maintained by the Spirit. The latter formed what became known as the Eastern Orthodox Church, which flourished in Greece, Russia, and Eastern Europe.

The Trinity – the belief in God as Father (Creator), Son (Jesus), and Holy Ghost (Spirit) is an important concept in the Orthodox Church. They also have priests and bishops, all of whom are men, and they can be married or single.

Worship: Services try to capture the wonder and mystery of heaven and usually include the use of icons (special religious artworks), incense, chanting, singing, and candles. Their worship always includes the celebration of the Eucharist (Communion).

Roman Catholic Church

This church traces its history back to New Testament times. According to tradition, the apostle Peter became the first bishop of Rome and he passed that responsibility and authority along to his successors right down to the present. The bishop of Rome is more commonly known as the Pope (currently John Paul II).

The Roman Catholic Church places a special emphasis on tradition and saints. Their clergy (priests, bishops and archbishops) are all men and cannot marry. Many Roman Catholics – clergy and laity, men and women – have been at the forefront of anti-poverty and justice movements.

Anglican Church (Church of England; Episcopal Church)

Christianity was present in Britain by about 200 CE and flourished among the Celtic peoples. Most British Christians considered the Pope as the head of the church until the 16th century when a combination of British nationalism and resentment against church taxation caused King Henry VIII to declare himself head of the church in England.

Anglican beliefs are quite similar to those of the Roman Catholic Church. However, priests and bishops can be married or single, and in many countries (including Canada and the USA), both women and men can be ordained.

Worship: Anglicans follow a prayer book for their worship, and usually celebrate Communion weekly. Some "high" churches burn incense and chant the Gospel and many prayers, while others are much less formal.

Baptists and Anabaptists

During the time of the Reformation (in the 16th century), a number of church leaders questioned the practice of infant baptism, preferring to baptize people who were old enough to make their own statement of faith (this is known as "believer's baptism"). These people became known as "Anabaptists" (from "ana" meaning "second" baptism). Out of this movement came our modern Anabaptist and Baptist churches. Clergy are usually male, although more women are becoming ministers in some Baptist and Anabaptist churches.

Anabaptists: Some groups, such as the Amish, Mennonites, and Hutterites chose to live simple lives in community. Among these groups there is a strong emphasis on peace and non-violence. Congregations are independent, making their own decisions about leadership, worship, etc. Although some Anabaptists still live in separate communities, most work at living out a simple lifestyle among mainstream society.

Baptists: The central focus of Baptist worship is usually the sermon. Communion is not celebrated often. Baptism (of those old enough to make a personal decision) is almost always by immersion.

Lutherans

In 1517, a German monk named Martin Luther challenged a number of practices in the Roman Catholic Church. This was the beginning of what came to be called the Reformation, in which a number of groups broke away from the Roman Catholic Church.

A major part of Luther's belief (which influenced many Protestant churches) was that only God's grace could save people; human beings did not have to do anything to earn God's salvation. Lutherans also place a great emphasis on scripture and creeds, rather than on tradition. In some branches of the Lutheran church, women as well as men can be pastors and bishops.

Worship: Lutheran worship generally combines strong preaching with the celebration of Communion. Confirmation is a very important process in Lutheran churches; preparation for this can often take two years.

Presbyterians

The Presbyterian Church was established in the 16th century by a French lawyer named John Calvin and Scottish clergyman named John Knox. Like Lutherans, Presbyterians believe that we are saved by God's grace and cannot earn salvation.

In place of bishops, the Presbyterian church is governed by courts or councils (called "presbyteries" from a Greek word meaning "elder"). The church is part of the World council of Reformed Churches. Both men and women can be ordained. A moderator presides over the meeting of all church courts including the yearly General Assembly of elected delegates.

Worship: Early Presbyterians believed in singing only the hymns of the Bible. Today many Presbyterian hymns are still based on the Psalms. Communion is celebrated at least 4 times a year. The sermon is an important part of Presbyterian worship services.

Christian Church (Disciples of Christ)

This denomination began in the USA when several smaller groups joined together. They are similar to Presbyterians and Congregationalists *(see United Church)* in belief and practice.

Worship: Communion is celebrated every time Disciples worship. It was a Disciple (Dr. Jesse Bader) who first encouraged the observance of a Worldwide Communion Sunday.

United Church of Canada

This church was formed in 1925 by a union of Methodists, Presbyterians, and Congregationalists. The Methodists were founded in the 1700s by an Anglican priest, John Wesley, who wanted people to take their Christian faith more seriously. Wesley encouraged Bible study, personal devotion, and acts of justice and kindness. The Congregationalists were English Christians who believed that all church authority ought to belong to the local congregation.

United Church ministers can be men or women. The moderator (national head of the church) can be a minister or lay person.

Worship: There is a wide variety of worship styles in United Church worship. Communion is usually celebrated once a month (often on the first Sunday).

Evangelical Churches

In Canada alone, there are about 3 million people who would consider themselves members of "evangelical" churches. Evangelical churches include Pentecostal, Charismatic, Fundamentalist, Reformed, Holiness, Alliance churches, etc. What these churches have in common is that members believe that the Bible is God's word to their churches, and all of humanity. Many take the Bible literally (for example, believing that God created the earth in 7 days). They also believe that a person is "born again" when he or she makes a personal commitment to follow Jesus.

Worship: This varies greatly among evangelical churches. However, a common thread is that the Bible is frequently quoted during worship. There is also a strong belief in God's personal relationship with each person.

Idea Page # Media: TV and Commercials

Group Check-in

Invite group members to use this formula to figure out their name if they were a TV soap opera star: combine your middle name and the name of a street you've lived on. Share the names for hilarious results!

Popular Jingles

Create a list of popular jingles (see examples below) or company/brand logos (e.g. the Nike "swoosh"). Have the youth work individually or in pairs to name as many of the products these jingles advertise as they can. Set a time limit. Award a silly prize for the person/pair who gets the most correct answers.

Examples

M'm, m'm...good! (Campbell's soup)
Obey your thirst. (Sprite)
Like a rock. (Ford trucks)
Don't leave home without it. (American Express)
Life tastes good. (Coke)
It just keeps going, and going, and going. (Eveready batteries)
We sell for less every day. (Wal-Mart)
Getting clean just got easier. (Tide laundry detergent)
Look good on your own terms. (Special K cereal)
Good to the last drop. (Maxwell House coffee)

Ad-Busting

Examine a few of the ads with popular jingles. What are these ads really trying to sell? How do they use images, words, or music to get us to buy? Design ads and satires that challenge the idea that we are what we wear, or that constant consumption is a good thing. Or examine some ads that spoof popular brands or products. What ideas are being challenged by these ads? How do these ads help us to think about our choices as consumers?

Remote Control Skits

Prepare for side-splitting sound bites with these skits! Divide into small groups or pairs. Give each an assignment to create a script for a first-aid program; a cooking show; an infomercial; a newscast about an animal escaping from the zoo. Assign one person the remote control; begin by pointing to one group, who begins reading their script. The laughs come when the viewer engages in a little "channel surfing," switching between programs.

Awareness-raising Collage Poster

Draw the outline of a body, or a television set, or question mark, on a strip of newsprint. Paste words and images cut from magazines inside the outline. Cut out and give it a title such as "Are you shaped by TV commercials?" You might wish to include statistics about television-watching habits and the money spent on advertising. Place this in a prominent location to raise awareness.

Media Influence Continuum

Discuss how media influence can be negative or positive (e.g. drinking and driving commercials). Stand on an imaginary line. Mark one end of the room "0" and the other end "10." If zero means "no influence" and ten means "major influence," place yourself on the line according to how much you think the media influences your (people your age) decisions about:

• Your clothing style.
• Your beliefs about God.
• Your choices of food/brands.
• Your views about marriage.
• Your choice to stay in school.
• Your career choice.
• Your attitude about alcohol and other drugs.
• Your views about the environment.
• Your views about the Middle East.

Did you know...?

- In 1950, only 10% of North American homes had a television set. By 1960 that percentage had grown to 90%. Today 99% of homes have a television; more families own a TV than a phone.
- North American children and adolescents spend 22–28 hours per week viewing television – more than any other activity except sleeping.
- The average person will watch more than 200,000 acts of violence, including 16,000 murders, before they are 18 years old.
- On average, North American teens view 2,000 beer and wine commercials per year.

Spirituality and TV

Stage a marathon of episodes of a favorite television program that deals with spirituality, such as *The Simpsons* or *Touched by an Angel*. Read the resource page **Spirituality and the Sitcoms** on page 67. Use this to spark discussion about the way God, heaven and hell, prayer and Christianity are portrayed on television.

Additional resources

The Gospel According to the Simpsons: The Spiritual Life of the World's Most Animated Family by Mark I. Pinsky (Louisville: Westminster John Knox Press, 2001)

The Power of Image (37 min., VHS)
Divided into five parts, this video will flood the viewer's senses with images from distant times and places as well as from television and Hollywood's manipulation of their power on our subconscious through the silver screen.

Watching TV (National Film Board of Canada, 5 min., 1994, VHS)
Available through some public libraries, this short animated film poses many profound questions about watching and responding to TV violence.

Strangers in the House (National Film Board of Canada, 52 min, 1997, VHS)
This film features interviews with media critics and TV-watching kids.

http://adbusters.org Check out the spoof ads at this website.

http://library.thinkquest.org/17067 Electric Snow is a student-created website geared toward students ages 12 to 18. It encourages youth to be aware of themselves and the way they are influenced by television.

Closing Worship

Ask a youth to lead the following meditation, inviting the whole group to read the words that are printed in bold, in unison.

In the beginning was the **Word**,
and the **Word** was with God,
and the **Word** was God.
And through the **Word** were made all living creatures,
birds, reptiles, insects, and people.
And everything was good.
A people created their own **words**.
Words of hurt and anger,
words of trickery and deceit,
words of bitterness and rejection,
words of lust and greed,
words by the millions.
So many **words**, so many.
Words were bought and sold, truth became a commodity.
People could no longer hear the word of **truth**,
the word of **hope**,
the word of **forgiveness**,
the word of **love**.
So into the babble of words God spoke,
a word which some found disturbing,
a word which some found embarrassing,
a word which some found liberating,
and God's word was "**Jesus**."

Prayer:
O God, every day we hear all sorts of messages about what's important –
messages from the media, from TV ads, or from newspapers,
all clamoring for our attention, saying, "Me, me, pay attention to me!"
Sometimes it's hard to figure out what's really important.
Help us, God, to pay attention to what matters most. Amen.

Spirituality and the Sitcoms

Touched By An Angel

Each week thousands of people tune in to be touched by an angel. Well, not one, but three angels to be exact: Andrew, Monica, and Tess on the popular evening drama *Touched By An Angel*. John Dye plays Andrew, the Angel of Death; Roma Downey plays Monica, the soft-hearted angel dispatched to Earth to help people facing crossroads in their lives. The two angels are watched over by Tess (played by Della Reese), the gruff but good-hearted supervisor angel, who steers both her trainees and their human "assignments" back on the right path.

Although all three actors are Christians, Roma Downey (who plays Monica) says she thinks *Touched By An Angel* is a spiritual show, not a religious one. "We don't support one denomination over another, or one religion over another," says John Dye. With all the violence, dishonesty, and explicit sexuality in prime-time television programs, the cast is conscious that the show's message is a crucial one. "When you watch television, it impresses you. And we're impressing upon their minds and hearts, bodies and beings that God is consciously aware of them and [that] God loves them," says Reese (who plays Tess).

Roma Downey says about the show's success, "I think we are helping to fill a void with *Touched By An Angel* by sending a positive message. It's letting people know that they are not alone." She attributes part of the series' success to how the angels themselves are defined. "We don't come into the situation and wave a fairy wand and make everything magically okay," she says, adding that her character in particular has a tendency to make mistakes.

Della Reese says her faith in God has been instrumental in getting her through a lot of rough times. "I don't mean [the kind of faith] when you say you believe in God or you go to church every Sunday, I'm not talking about that. I'm talking about the real deal. When you really believe in God, it gives you a courage, a confidence that enables you to meet the things coming. Things don't stop coming now, don't misunderstand me. But when you really trust in God, you have a courage. You see it coming, you meet it, and you keep on trucking!"

The show draws inspiration for episodes from situations the cast and writers have experienced,

or other real life stories like that of the artist Richard Bunkall, or a young couple whose two children have sickle cell anemia. Williamson reflects on how she became involved with the show when CBS approached her to produce the drama: "You look back over 7 years and see how God put everything in place, Della, Roma, John and me. Everybody is here for a reason, there is no question about it." Actor John Dye agrees: "As my mom always says, there is no such thing as a coincidence. It's just God remaining anonymous."

You can find a guide to past and upcoming episodes of *Touched By An Angel* at http://www.touched.com

The Simpsons

President George Bush Sr. once denounced it; his wife Barbara called it dumb. Conservative Christians have condemned it. But despite criticism, *The Simpsons* is one of the longest running, funniest, most irreverent, and, according to some religious leaders, the most theologically relevant show on television today. During the same two-week period in early 2001, *The Simpsons* appeared on the covers of *Christianity Today* and the *Christian Century*, two magazines at opposite ends of the theological spectrum.

In his book *The Gospel According to the Simpsons: The Spiritual Life of the World's Most Animated Family*, Mark Pinsky looks at the use of God, Jesus, heaven and hell, the Bible, prayer in the Simpson household, the next-door evangelist Ned Flanders, and the town's church and pastor, Rev. Lovejoy.

"In the Simpson household, prayer most frequently takes the form of blessings at mealtimes – including grace over takeout fast food and, on at least one occasion, in a restaurant. Often, the prayers are perfunctory, as Bart's 'Rub a dub, dub, thanks for the grub,' or Homer's equally succinct but barely more reverent, 'Good drink, good meat, good God, let's eat.' On one occasion Bart seems to speak the unspeakable: 'Dear God, we paid for all this stuff ourselves, so thanks for nothing.' In the early 1990s, the young child of a member of Willow Creek Community Church, the megachurch in

Barrington, Ill., offered a version of this grace at the family table, shocking his father. The man complained to a minister, Lee Strobel, saying that the child was prohibited from watching *The Simpsons*, but picked up the prayer from a commercial advertising an upcoming episode.

"Strobel, a former journalist at the *Chicago Tribune* who became a teaching pastor at Willow Creek, used the incident to introduce a sermon titled, 'What Jesus Would Say to Bart Simpson.' Strobel explained that the episode's grace was 'an exaggerated look at life from a kid's perspective, with a kernel of truth at its core.' Because Bart is so uninhibited, he says things that other people only think. When he prays, 'Why should we thank you, God – we bought this ourselves,' people recoil in horror. Yet isn't he just expressing a sentiment that a lot of people secretly harbor? They'd never say it, but don't many people live their lives with the attitude that they've earned what they've received and that God really has nothing to do with it?

"The Simpsons are 'a family where God has a place at the table,' said Robert Thompson of Syracuse University in a newspaper interview. Homer gives thanks for his job. One evening he takes the opportunity to thank God 'most of all for nuclear power, which has yet to cause a single, proven fatality, at least in this country.' And, at Thanksgiving, 'we especially thank you for nuclear power, the cleanest, safest energy source there is, except solar, which is just a pipe dream.' Yet the family sometimes acknowledges during grace that its blessings are mixed and, this being *The Simpsons*, things simply spin out of control. After this particular Thanksgiving turns into a disaster, Homer loses it, offering thanks 'for the occasional moments of peace and love our family's experienced... well, not today. You saw what happened. Oh Lord, be honest! Are we the most pathetic family in the world, or what?' (His sister-in-law Selma comments, 'Worst prayer yet.') By the conclusion of the episode the conflicts are resolved and, as the sound track plays 'We Gather Together,' the family eats turkey sandwiches. 'Oh Lord,' Homer says, 'on this blessed day, we thank Thee for giving our family one more crack at togetherness.'

"If the Simpson's next door neighbor Ned Flanders is an exemplar of evangelical Christianity, Lisa represents the essence of Bible-believing, mainline denominations, with their commitment to a socially conscious gospel and rational, religious humanism. She rejects the faith healing of a Pentecostal preacher at a tent revival as 'mumbo-jumbo.' In her own way, she speaks for a Christianity as envisioned by many modern believers. Consider the ways in which Lisa's words and actions parallel those of Jesus of the Bible:

"Lisa supports the poor, the powerless and the downtrodden, and is critical of the rich. Her goal is to do good in the world, to alleviate suffering and, when necessary, to guilt others into doing the same. She backs the rights of striking workers in Springfield and, in the years when South Africa had a white-ruled government, she had anti-apartheid posters hanging in her bedroom...In another episode, her grandfather, Abe Simpson, unexpectedly inherits $100,000 and wonders what to do with it. Lisa urges him to give it to the needy.

"Lisa questions the conventional wisdom, regardless of how unpopular such questioning might be. Like the ancient prophets, she is a compulsive truth-teller, seeming to take a perverse joy in whom and how she offends...It seems the more inopportune the occasion, the more likely she is to speak out, to speak truth to power. As Little Miss Springfield, Lisa is asked to sing *The Star Spangled Banner* before a football game. She uses the occasion to announce, 'Before I sing the national anthem, I'd like to say that college football drains funds that are badly needed for education and the arts.' Her subsequent denunciation of the tobacco company that sponsors the Little Miss Springfield contest costs her the tiara.

"Lisa believes in the concept of stewardship of the earth and its resources, and defends the rights of God's lesser beings. A committed environmentalist and vegetarian, she opposes the needless killing of creatures – including snakes at Springfield's annual Whacking Day.

"Lisa takes pity on scorned individuals, offering solace and affection for the unloved. Her concern is not only for the collective good. She tries to transform a playground bully and all around bad boy named Nelson Muntz, whose parents are in prison, with her puppy love. She takes pity on dim-witted Ralph Wiggum, who she notices has not received a single Valentine, by changing the name on one of her cards to his."

Excerpted from *The Gospel According to the Simpsons* by Mark I. Pinsky. (Louisville: Westminster John Knox Press, 2001) Reprinted with permission.

Visit http://thesimpsons.com for a complete episode guide.

Pop Culture:
Movies & Music

Group Check-in

If your life was a movie, what would your music soundtrack be? Take turns explaining your choice to the other group members.

Name That Tune

Print the titles of well-known songs or hymns on slips of paper. Divide into two teams. One person from each team is chosen to hum the tune while other team members try to guess what song it is. Use a timer and allow only one minute for teams to guess. If the team is unable to name it correctly, the other team has a chance to guess. Award points for each song a team guesses correctly. Some suggested songs: *Jesus Loves Me, Amazing Grace, Away in a Manger, All Things Bright and Beautiful, Go Tell It on the Mountain, Joy to the World, Let There Be Peace on Earth, This Is the Day the Lord Has Made.*

Do you have a favorite hymn or song? Why is it your favorite? Do you know any hymns that are favorites of your parents or grandparents (or older members of the congregation)? What do you think of the music in our church? If you could change something about the music in our church, what would you change?

Spirituality and Music

Ask members to bring a copy of a song that is inspirational to them and a photocopy of its lyrics if it has any. Listen to the songs, following the lyrics, and then discuss the song and its meaning. The person who brought the song goes last, sharing why it is inspirational for them.

The Story behind the Music

Research and share some of the stories behind well-known hymns, such as *What a Friend We Have in Jesus.* Then try your hand at writing your own! Choose a theme or topic and brainstorm, recording on newsprint any ideas or words that come to mind connected to the topic. Choose a well-known tune (e.g. a Christmas carol or *Kum Ba Yah*). Using words and ideas from the brainstorming, begin writing lines for the song. Encourage everyone to participate. As you come up with lines, keep singing the tune to make sure the words fit. Print out the words to the final version and perform it, with rhythm instruments if you wish! For example, here is a verse from an Advent song written to the tune of *This Is My Father's World*:

Fear not, you hungry child, you homeless refugee,
You battered woman, burdened down – God came to set you free.
For God's own Son was poor; He cried and suffered, too.
God's grace astounds, God's love abounds, for people just like you.

What a Friend We Have in Jesus
Words by Joseph Scriven, 1819–1886
Music by Charles C. Converse, 1832–1918

Joseph Scriven was born in 1819 of prosperous parents in Dublin, Ireland. Joseph learned early in life to give his griefs to the Lord. On the night before he was to be married, his bride was found accidentally drowned. Following her tragic death, Scriven decided to migrate to Canada and start a new life in Port Hope, Ontario. A deeply religious person, Scriven became known as the "Good Samaritan of Port Hope." It is said that he gave freely of his limited possessions, even sharing the clothing from his own body, if necessary, and never once refused to help anyone who needed it. Ira Sankey tells in his writings of the man who, seeing Scriven in the streets of Port Hope, with his sawbuck and saw, asked, "Who is that man? I want him to work for me." The answer was, "You cannot get that man; he saws wood only for poor widows and sick people who cannot pay." Scriven wrote the words to *What a Friend We Have in Jesus* for his mother, upon learning she was seriously ill, because he was unable to return to Dublin to be with her. He wrote a letter of comfort to her, enclosing the words of this text. Some time later when he himself was ill, a friend who came to visit him saw the poem. The friend read it with keen interest and asked Scriven if he had written the words. Scriven, with typical modesty, replied, "The Lord and I did it between us." Some years later, Charles C. Converse composed music to accompany the words to the hymn we know as *What a Friend We Have in Jesus.*

"Holy"wood Squares

For this fun *Hollywood Squares*-style game, prepare 20–25 questions (true/false, multiple choice or open-ended) about the movie you are going to view – trivia about the actors, the setting, characters, or plot.

You will need: nine pieces of poster board, each marked with an "X" on one side and an "O" on the other side

Instructions: Choose two volunteers to be the contestants ("X" and "O"). Invite nine people to be the "celebrity players." The nine sit or stand in three rows of three, holding a piece of poster board. The game leader asks a question and a contestant chooses one of the players to direct the question to. The object is for contestants to guess if the player is giving the right answer or guessing/bluffing. If the contestant guesses correctly (either by agreeing or disagreeing with the player), the player turns the appropriate side of the poster-board "square." The first contestant to get three squares in a row vertically, horizontally, or diagonally wins.

Spirituality and Movies

Movies can provide insightful and inspirational material for youth group discussions. Some may even provide glimpses of the emerging kingdom of God. See pages 72–74 for a list of thought-provoking films on some of the themes of this book and other topics. Visit the websites listed on this page (see **Additional Resources**) for other recommended films on spiritual themes, synopses, reviews, and ratings. Read the section on **Videos and Youth Groups** on page 17 for important information on copyright laws. As you begin planning your program, read the **Tips for Using a Video As an Educational Tool with Youth** on page 71.

Additional resources

http://www.hollywoodjesus.com This site, dedicated to spirituality and the movies, includes reviews of current films and message boards where people debate their views of subjects and themes presented in the movies.

http://www.beliefnet.com Features interviews with celebrities, such as U2's Bono, about their beliefs.

http://www.abc-em.org/resources/yadult-movie.cfm At the time of publication, this site offered free Bible studies based on movies such as *Simon Birch, Pleasantville, A Bug's Life.*

http://www.moviemom.com Nell Minow writes about movies, television, the Internet, and parenting. Her site includes reviews of films currently in the theatres and on video, including rating, suggested audience, and notes on content (sexual references, drug abuse, violence, and tolerance/diversity). Her more recent reviews include some questions that could be the basis for discussion.

Praying the Movies: Daily Meditations from Classic Films by Edward McNulty (Louisville: Geneva Press, 2001). A collection of devotions – each containing a passage from scripture, a description of a scene from a popular film, a meditation, and questions to encourage reflection – based on films such as *Star Wars, Dead Man Walking, The Spitfire Grill,* and *Schindler's List.*

Reel to Real: Making the Most of the Movies with Youth (Nashville: Abingdon Press, 2000). Explores themes such as spirituality, friendship, honesty, and love through popular films. Outlines include the film's rating, cautions, a brief synopsis, discussion questions, and other activities. If you only have time to view clips, key scenes are identified with VCR counter cues. Conservative to liberal theology.

Closing Worship

O God,
In this Season after Epiphany,
we give thanks for the ways we see you revealed in the world –
through the seasons of nature, through music, through people we encounter, even through technology.
Help us to spread your love to others. Amen.

Tips for Using a Video As an Educational Tool with Youth

• Screen the video carefully beforehand. Do not rely on others' recommendations or a vague recollection of having seen the film yourself and thinking it was suitable.

• Consider the ages and developmental stages of the youth audience. Is the subject matter appropriate? Will it interest them? What is your purpose in showing the video? Imagine some of your group members going home and giving a synopsis of the film to a parent. How might parents react? If you have a support group made up of parents who have youth in the group, make sure they understand why you are choosing to view this film and what you hope to accomplish with it. They can help reassure other parents   and adults in the congregation who might be skeptical.

• If you want the group to view only part of the film, preview it on the VCR that you will use with the program. Make note of key "clips" so that you can fast-forward to these scenes, using the start-end times and your VCR counter. Showing a few clips may be a good compromise when a thought-provoking film contains scenes unsuitable for youth viewers. Be prepared to provide an account of the missing story parts so that the narrative continuity is maintained.

• Create a list of questions to guide discussion. Write these on newsprint and display them before beginning the video. Encourage youth to refer to them from time to time. Alternatively, photocopy the list for each member, asking them to record their own responses and discuss them with a partner when the movie ends. A list of questions can guide youth while viewing the movie and increase their awareness as an audience. If you are renting videos from a church outlet, ask for a list of discussion questions and a copy of the study guide whenever these are available.

• Introduce the video to the youth. Give them an idea of the film's subject matter. If the movie contains scenes that might make some youth uncomfortable, warn them about these. (Movies that touch on "disturbing" or difficult subjects do not necessarily need to be excluded. Youth can be given information to help them choose whether or not to watch them.)

• Allow time to discuss the film after viewing it. And conclude with a devotional moment. This might include a passage from scripture and a brief prayer.

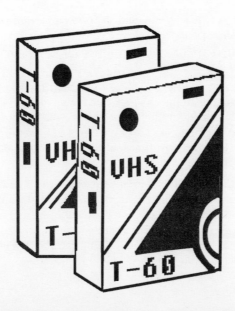

Recommended Films on Themes in This Book

All Saints

Gandhi (Columbia TriStar, 188 min., 1982. Starring Ben Kingsley, Candice Bergen)
This film tells one of the most important stories of the 20th century, that of India's struggle to free itself, spearheaded by one of the most extraordinary men of all time, Mahatma Gandhi. His work to free his country from British rule using peaceful means gives hope and inspiration.

Romero (Vidmark Entertainment, 102 min., 1989. Starring Raul Julia, Richard Jordan)
Based on the true story of Oscar Romero, who became archbishop of El Salvador in 1980 during the dark days of a military regime. Romero is transformed by the suffering of the poor to become the "voice of the voiceless." His opposition to the violence he sees earns him the love of his people and eventually leads to his assassination. This is powerful story of compassion, Christian conviction, and the intolerance of the powerful towards social change.

Cry Freedom (Universal Pictures, 154 min., 1987. Starring Denzel Washington, Kevin Kline)
The gripping story of Steve Biko, a black leader fighting against apartheid in South Africa, as seen through the eyes of Donald Woods, editor of the East London (South Africa) *Daily Dispatch*. Through an emissary, Biko arranges to meet Woods, who has written sanctimonious editorials describing Biko as a black racist. Eventually the two men become friends, and Woods sees black life in South Africa first-hand.

Christmas on Division Street (120 min., 1999. Starring Hume Cronyn, Fred Savage)
A made-for-TV movie based on the true story of Trevor Ferrel who helped destitute people on the streets of Philadelphia and transformed the way many people see the homeless. This is a story about love, friendship, and compassion.

City of Joy (Columbia Tristar, 135 min., 1992. Starring Patrick Swayze, Pauline Collins, Om Puri)
A young American surgeon leaves everything his life stands for to travel to India to "escape." Through a series of events he is thrust into the melee of Calcutta and finds himself in the "City of Joy." This poignant drama touches on many themes including, friendship, prejudice, and the call to serve others.

Stereotypes and Prejudice

The Mighty (Miramax, 106 min.,1999. Starring Kieran Culkin, Elden Ratliff, Sharon Stone)
Max lives with his grandparents since his violent father is in prison. At school, he is harassed by bullies. Max's prospects change when Kevin, a physically deformed youth, becomes Max's reading tutor. Soon they are bonded in their yearning to be modern Knights of the Roundtable. This film celebrates the imagination and friendship that enables these two outsiders to transcend their disabilities, loneliness, and familial problems.

Mask (Universal Pictures, 120 min., 1985. Starring Cher, Eric Stoltz)
Based on a true story of a single mother trying to provide a normal life for her son Rocky, who suffers from a deforming, and ultimately fatal craniofacial disease. This touching drama explores how love can overcome prejudice and fear to reveal the inner beauty of a person.

Breakfast Club (Universal Pictures, 92 min., 1985. Starring Emilio Estevez, Judd Nelson, Ally Sheedy, Molly Ringwald, Anthony Michael Hall)
Five students – Allison, a weirdo; Brian, a nerd; John, a misfit; Claire, a popular prom queen; and Andy, a jock – are forced to spend the day in Saturday detention. At first they think they don't have much in common, but as each begins to see the others apart from their stereotypes they soon learn that behind the exterior they are all the same.

Racial Discrimination

American History X (New Line Cinema, 117 min., 1998. Starring Ed Norton, Edward Furlong, Beverly D'Angelo)
Danny Vineyard idolizes his older brother Derek, who is serving time in prison for brutally murdering an African-American boy. While in prison, Derek's racial views are transformed. Three years later he returns home to find Danny has become a skinhead just like him.

The Long Walk Home (Cineplex Odeon Home Video, 106 min., 1987. Starring Whoopi Goldberg, Sissy Spacek)
The story of Odessa Carter, a black maid to an upperclass white family in 1956 in Montgomery, Alabama, during the height of the Civil Rights Movement in the United States. Sparked by the actions of Rosa Parks, an African-American woman who refused to give up her seat on a crowded bus, the bus boycotts by African-Americans in the US resulted in the Supreme Court decision to change segregation laws that required African-American people to sit at the back of the bus.

Remember the Titans (Walt Disney, 113 min., 2000. Starring Denzel Washington, Will Patton, Wood Harris)
This movie is about the real-life integration of a Virginia high school football team in 1971, 17 years after the Brown vs. Board of Education decision ended the legal segregation of black and white students in United States' schools. As the white T.C. Williams players are confronted with not only a whole new set of black players, but a black coach, Herman Boone, they form friendships that transcend racial differences. The movie tackles the issue of racism and other forms of prejudice such as sexism and homophobia.

AIDS

The Ryan White Story
A made-for-TV movie that tells the true story of Ryan White, a young hemophiliac who contracted AIDS through a blood transfusion. When the people in the town he lived in learned he had the disease, Ryan and his family became targets of discrimination based on people's fear and ignorance. Ryan courageously fought for his own rights and the right of people with AIDS to be treated with compassion.

Philadelphia (Columbia TriStar, 125 min., 1993. Starring Denzel Washington, Tom Hanks)
A gay lawyer stricken with AIDS seeks assistance from a homophobic personal injury attorney when a prestigious Philadelphia law firm fires him for incompetence. This film explores the effect of AIDS on family and friends and the fear that fuels prejudice.

The Cure (MCA Universal, 99 min., 1995. Starring Joseph Mazzello, Brad Renfro, Annabella Sciorra)
Eleven-year-old Dexter and his mom move to a new town and are quickly shunned when it's learned Dexter has AIDS. A surprising friendship develops between Dexter and Erik, a lonely, latchkey bully who lives next door. After the twosome read a tabloid that says a New Orleans doctor has found a cure for AIDS they set out on a magical, often hilarious journey of hope that changes both boys' lives forever.

In the Gloaming (HBO, 67 min., 1997. Starring Glenn Close, Robert Sean Leonard)
A son with AIDS comes home to die and confronts his family's fear, guilt, and misconceptions.

The Bible

Stigmata (MGM, 103 min., 1999. Starring Patricia Arquette, Gabriel Byrne)
Stigmata – bleeding wounds of the head, hands, back, and feet that resemble the five wounds of Christ on the cross – have appeared over the centuries on the bodies of deeply religious people all over the world. Although they are unexplained phenomena, one thing has always been true: they appear only on the bodies of believers. When they appear on a woman who has no religious affiliation, the Vatican sends an investigator to uncover the truth. This film can be used to explore ideas about religious experiences, God's call, and atheism.

The Seventh Sign (Columbia TriStar, 97 min., 1988. Starring Demi Moore)
Although it is based on a literal view of the Book of Revelation as a prophecy of the end of the world, this story has a powerful ending. It could provoke some good conversation about sin, salvation, and God's mercy – and the interpretation of scripture.

The Truman Show (Paramount Pictures, 103 min., 1998. Starring Jim Carrey)
Truman lives in the town of Seahaven (really the construction of creator-director Christof, the omnipotent, omnipresent god-like director that controls this televised, human-made Paradise). Seahaven is a perfect world – a Garden of Eden – where there is no crime, no bad weather, everyone has money, the homes all look the same. Truman is unaware that his life, "The Truman Show," is the longest running, most popular documentary-soap opera in history, until one day a studio light falls from the sky. This movie is a wonderful allegory that touches on the themes of free choice, the nature of God, and our relationship to God.

Pleasantville (Alliance Atlantis, 124 min., 1999. Starring Tobey Macguire, Reese Witherspoon, Jeff Daniels)
This Leave it to Beaver-esque town couldn't be more different from the trouble-plagued real world that David and Jennifer, fraternal twins of divorced parents, live in. When the two are transported into the utopian world of the television show Pleasantville, the mythical 1950s meet the all too-real 1990s. This Garden of Eden story explores free choice and innocence lost through "the knowledge of Good and Evil." The ending of the film presents an interesting question: "Where do we go from here?"

Faith

Leap of Faith (Malofilm, 108 min., 1992. Starring Steve Martin, Debra Winger, Lucas Haas)
Jonas Nightingale is a fraudulent faith healer who uses all the tricks in the book to con people into giving him money. When he and his entourage become stranded in a small town, Jonas undergoes a transformation when he meets a handicapped boy who believes in him. This film can be a good discussion starter about beliefs about healing and miracles.

Keeping the Faith (Touchstone, 128 min., 2000. Starring Ben Stiller, Edward Norton, Jenna Elfman)
Jake, a Jewish Rabbi, and Brian, a Roman Catholic priest, grow up together in New York City and are both interested in each other's religion. A reunion many years later with once-childhood friend Anna sparks chaos. This humorous film examines the important roles of religion and spirituality in a person's life and what happens when these strong beliefs are put to the test.

Chocolat (Miramax, 121 min., 2000. Starring Juliette Binoche, Johnny Depp, Judi Dench)
Single mother Vianne Rocher and her six-year-old daughter move into town and open a chocolate shop just as Lent is beginning – a time of traditional fasting. Her ability to perceive her customers' private desires and to satisfy them with just the right confection coaxes the villagers to abandon themselves to temptation. A battle thus begins between Vianne and the town's self-appointed moral guardian, the Comte de Reynoud. But Vianne's warm personality and magical chocolate transform the townspeople. This film can spark interesting discussion about the difference between being good and being pious, the goodness of creation, and temptation.

The Mission (Warner Bros, 126 min., 1986. Starring Robert DeNiro, Jeremy Irons)
Father Gabriel, a Spanish Jesuit priest, goes into the South American jungle to build a mission in the hope of bringing Christianity to the Indians of the region. Mendoza, a slave trader, kills his brother in a fit of rage and is befriended by Fr. Gabriel who takes him to his mission. There Mendoza finds redemption, forgiveness, and peace.

Simon Birch (Buena Vista, 110 min., 1998. Starring Ian Michael Smith, Joseph Mazzello, Ashley Judd)
Simon is a pint-sized curmudgeon who believes he has been put on earth as "God's instrument." As all prophets do, Simon gets into trouble by not keeping quiet about his faith, to the consternation of everyone who hears his squeaky little voice declare his belief in God's plans for him. The film touches on the themes of friendship, acceptance, and the resilience of faith.

Balance

Big (Trimark, 102 min., 1988. Starring Tom Hanks)
Twelve-year-old Josh Baskin drops a quarter into an old-fashioned fortune-telling machine and tells the genie inside, "I wish I was big." The next morning he awakens to find himself trapped in the body of an adult. Josh takes a job as a computer specialist at MacMillan Toys and his boys-world view transforms the adults around him who've lost contact with the kid inside them.

The Kid (Disney, 108 min., 2000. Starring Bruce Willis, Spencer Breslin, Lily Tomlin)
Russ Duritz is a cold, high-priced image consultant who meets his younger self when the chubby and adorable Rusty mysteriously shows up and helps him reconnect to his childhood dreams and his true self. This film explores the themes of self-respect, bullying, and "being yourself."

The Family Man (Universal Pictures, 100 min., 2000. Starring Nicholas Cage, Teo Leoni)
Jack Campbell is a self-obsessed man who is perfectly happy with his life the way it is. He loves money and his fast-paced lifestyle. When he is mysteriously catapulted into the life he chose not to have – a life in the New Jersey suburbs, married to his college sweetheart, with two small children, and a job selling tires – he thinks it is his worst nightmare, but soon discovers aspects of himself he's been missing. The film explores the themes of selfishness, materialism, and sacrifice.

Death/Life after Death

Flatliners (Columbia Tristar, 114 min., 1990. Starring Julia Roberts, Kiefer Sutherland, Kevin Bacon)
Five medical students experiment with bringing each other back from "near death experiences" only to be faced with unresolved issues and relationships from this life. This suspenseful drama presents interesting ideas about death/the afterlife, sin, and redemption.

The Sixth Sense (Buena Vista, 107 min., 1999. Starring Bruce Willis, Haley Joel Osment)
Dr. Malcolm Crowe, a child psychologist takes on the case of Cole Sear, a nine-year-old boy who seems to be suffering from visual hallucinations, paranoia, and schizophrenia. Eventually Cole tells Dr. Crowe that he sees ghosts and is terrified by them. Later, the boy learns that the dead have chosen him to help them deliver messages to those they love. This epiphany holds great meaning for Cole and the doctor.

Ghost (Malofilm, 128 min., 1990. Starring Patrick Swayze, Demi Moore, Whoopi Goldberg)
When Sam is murdered by a thief in a dark alley, he finds himself trapped as a ghost and realizes that his death was no accident. He must warn his wife Molly about the danger that she is in. But as a ghost he cannot be seen or heard by the living, and so he tries to communicate with Molly through Oda Mae Brown, a psychic who doesn't even realize that her powers are real. The film can be a discussion starter about beliefs about life after death, heaven and hell, and the paranormal.

Identity/Self-Esteem

Galaxy Quest (Dreamworks, 102 min., 1999. Starring Tim Allen, Sigourney Weaver)
Former stars of a cheesy Star Trek-style show that ended nearly 20 years ago are whisked into space by a group of aliens who received the television transmissions of the program's reruns and thought they were documentaries. The aliens believe the crew can defeat their all-too-real adversary, Sarris. To be so loved is transforming for the crew, who go from self-centeredness to other-centeredness, and rise up to become their best selves. A humorous parable about human worth, identity, and self-esteem.

Billy Elliot (Universal Pictures, 110 min., 2000. Starring Jamie Bell, Julie Walters, Jamie Driven)
Billy Elliot is an 11-year-old boy from an English mining community who uses ballet as an outlet for all the mixed feelings of anger, loss, and rebellion stirring in his adolescent soul. Heeding the advice of his deceased mother – to always be himself – he turns all his yearning into a passionate commitment to dance. This film can be a discussion starter about finding one's own identity and overcoming sexual stereotypes.

Can't Buy Me Love (Buena Vista, 95 min., 1987. Starring Patrick Dempsey, Amanda Peterson)
Ronald Miller is a nerd, an outcast, a member of the wrong crowd at school, who makes a deal with one of the most popular girls in school to help him break into the "cool" clique. He offers her $1,000 to pretend to be his girlfriend for a month. It succeeds, but he soon learns that the price of popularity may be higher than he expected. This film explores the issues of popularity, friendship, and self-esteem.

Made in Whose Image?
(Body image/self-esteem)

Group Check-in

Pass around a roll of toilet paper with no other explanation than to "tear off as much as you want." Hand out fine-tipped markers or ballpoint pens. Ask the youth to write one self-affirmation on each square, such as something they are good at or something they like about themselves. They don't need to share what they've written, but discuss: Was this hard to do?

Talents Auction

You will need: play money
Instructions: Write the following descriptions on separate squares of paper: good at art, good at speaking, good at writing, good at sports, good at being a friend, good at remembering, good at solving problems, good at telling stories/jokes, good at music, good at acting/drama.

Give everyone an equal amount of play money. Explain that you will be auctioning off different abilities that you have written on squares of paper. Everyone can bid however much they want until their money runs out. The ability is awarded to the person with the highest bid. Read out the abilities one by one and auction them off.

Afterwards discuss:

• Which talents or abilities were considered the most valuable? Why?

• Which ones did not get a good price?

• Which ones would you most like to have if you could have your pick of any of these abilities? Why?

• Which talents might God think are important? Do you think God considers that some are more important than others? Why or why not?

Ad Critique

Divide the group into pairs or groups of three. Provide each group with a copy of the **Ad Assignment** from page 77 and a men's or women's fashion magazine (e.g. *Glamour, Flare, Vanity Fair, Gentlemen's Quarterly*). Allow 2–5 minutes for groups to flip through their magazine and choose an ad. Then give groups another 10–15 minutes to complete the rest of the assignment. Invite groups to share the ad they chose and describe what they think is going on in the picture. Afterwards, discuss together: How has this assignment changed the way you view ads?

Oscar Party

The Academy Awards are held each spring to recognize distinction in the movie picture industry. Why not host your own Oscar night? Invite the youth to come in their best clothes. Serve fancy snacks. Award trophies for "Best Supporting Actress," "Best Costume Design," "Special Effects," or give a "Lifetime Achievement Award" to long-time members who may be graduating. Encourage acceptance speeches and take lots of photos.

Peer Pressure Continuum

What do the words "peer pressure" mean to you? Describe some situations where you have experienced peer pressure with good results and with bad results. Stand on an imaginary line. Mark one end of the room "0" and the other end "10." If zero means "no influence" and ten means "major influence," place yourself on the line depending on how much you think peer pressure affects your decisions about:

• Who you are friends with
• Your choice of girlfriend or boyfriend
• Your clothing style
• What music you listen to
• Whether you drink
• Whether you smoke
• If you go to church
• Whether you stay in school
• Who you go to grad with

Did you know…?

- Models, who 20 years ago weighed 8% less than an average woman, today weigh 23% less.
- Psychological studies have found that three minutes spent looking at pictures of such models in magazines caused 70% of women to feel depressed, guilty, and shameful.
- More than 50% of 10-year-old girls say they have tried a "diet."
- The average North American is exposed to over 3,000 advertisements a day and watches three years worth of television ads over the course of a lifetime.

Body Image Collage

Have a volunteer lie down on a long strip of banner paper and trace the outline of their body. Invite group members to look through magazines for images and words that represent messages about body image that the media gives us. Glue these to the paper to create a collage. Give the collage a title such as "Made in Whose Image?" or "What's shaping you?" and display it in a location where others can see it and reflect on it. You might include a Surgeon General's Warning such as "Reading fashion magazines can be hazardous to your health and confidence."

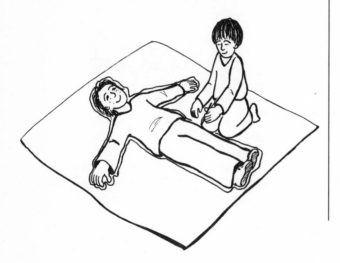

Additional resources

Can't Buy My Love: How Advertising Changes the Way We Think and Feel by Jean Kilbourne (New York: Simon & Schuster, 2001)
A fascinating exposé of how advertising affects young people in particular by offering false promises of rebellion, connection, and control.
Still Killing Us Softly (National Film Board of Canada, VHS, 32 minutes, 1992)
Jean Kilbourne, Ed.D., gets us to see ads with a new understanding of their power to distort our image of ourselves and others. Although this film is quite dated, the message is still relevant.
http://www.about-face.org A terrific website that combats negative and distorted images of women. Includes addresses of fashion magazines for letter-writing campaigns.

Closing Worship

Place computer or music CDs in a basket. Invite each person to take one. As they study their reflection, invite them to consider: What image of yourself do you carry around with you? Study your face, your looks, your style. But what's on the inside that can't be seen in the mirror?

Prayer:

Creator God, you have made each of us unique and special,
but when we see our differences we usually don't like them.
We label people "weird" and "strange" instead of accepting them for who they are.
Thank you for the people who see us as unique individuals
and who encourage us to be ourselves.
Help us to accept and encourage each other.
Amen.

Ad Assignment

Choose an ad from your magazine. As a group, look at it carefully and discuss what you see. Advertisers use a variety of techniques in ads to get us to pay attention or to convince us to buy something. Consider the message the ad conveys as you answer the following questions.

Consider...

• Is there any significance to the camera angle?

• What is the focus of the ad? What are your eyes drawn to first?

• What is going on in the ad?

• Is sex being used to sell this product?

• Is violence depicted, or suggested, in this ad?

• What emotions are portrayed in the ad? What emotion do you think this ad is trying to make you feel?

• What product is the ad trying to sell? Is it difficult to detect what product is being advertised?

• What problem does the ad suggest will be resolved by this product?

• If there are people in the ad, what ethnic groups do they represent?

• Are any of the people in the ad presented as objects (e.g. a person on all fours presented as a table)?

• What is the age of the models in the ad? Are any of them made to look younger than they are? Or older than they are?

• What underlying messages are conveyed by color, body language, or words in the ad?

• What attitudes does the ad suggest about sex, love, relationships, or gender roles (male and female)?

• Does the ad trivialize people's needs, fears, or rights?

Section D:

Season of Lent

Mood and Flavor of the Season

The Season of Lent is 40 days (and six Sundays) long, stretching from Ash Wednesday to Holy Saturday. Our English word *Lent* comes from the word "lengthen." In the Northern Hemisphere, Lent takes place as the days lengthen into spring. The liturgical color for Lent is purple, indicating a time of repentance. In Lent we take stock, both of ourselves and of our society. We reflect on our efforts to implement the values of peace, community, and equality of all before God.

Special Days

Ash Wednesday marks the beginning of the Season of Lent. Some churches have a brief service either on Shrove Tuesday or early on Wednesday morning. It may include the ritual imposition of ashes. Traditionally, the ashes that are placed on our foreheads in the sign of the cross are the ashes from the burning of the previous year's Palm Sunday branches or palm crosses. This ritual reminds us of our own mortality and need for repentance, both as individuals and as communities. Ashes symbolize mourning and humility; when the Hebrews mourned, they put dust or ashes on their heads and wore sackcloth as signs of humility. The ashes placed on our foreheads on Ash Wednesday remind us of the many things in our world that are not as God wants.

Holy Week begins with Passion or Palm Sunday commemorating the triumphant entry of Jesus into Jerusalem. Semitic people have always regarded the palm tree as a tree of honor; in Jesus' day it marked the place where shepherds could find water for their flocks. Even today the branches of palm trees are placed on the graves of some Semitic people to symbolize eternal life.

Holy Week includes Maundy Thursday or Holy Thursday when we remember the Last Supper. People in many churches prepare together and celebrate a traditional Jewish Seder meal on this evening. The term "Maundy" comes from the Latin *mandatum*, which means "commandment." Scripture describes Jesus washing his disciples' feet at the Last Supper as a demonstration of how everyone – both servant and master – is to be treated equally (John 13:16). Then he commanded them to love one another (John 13:34). In English tradition, on this day the monarch distributes alms – food, clothing, and money – to the poor. As in early centuries, in some places today clergy symbolically wash the feet of parishioners on this day.

Holy Week culminates in Good Friday. Special worship services are held to remember Jesus' crucifixion. Why do we call such a painful day "good"? One suggestion is that "good" represents a vowel shift from an older form of "God's Friday." The change from God's Friday to Good Friday might parallel the one from "God be wi' ye" (God be with ye) to "goodbye." By calling this day Good Friday, we also acknowledge that God's love overcame the evil in the world that crucified Jesus, and transformed it into good for the whole world. The author of the Gospel of John affirmed this with these words: "The light shines in the darkness, and the darkness has never put it out" (John 1:5). A traditional observance on Good Friday is called the Tenebrae Service. This solemn observance of the Lord's Supper began in the fourth century. The service involved the extinguishing of candles as a reminder of the darkness that covered the earth after the crucifixion of Jesus Christ (Luke 23:44–45). The word *tenebrae* means "darkness." The service usually begins in silence and ends in almost total darkness. The candles that are gradually extinguished during the service symbolize the gradual falling away and denial of the disciples and friends of Jesus.

The Season of Lent ends on Holy Saturday, a day when many Christians keep an Easter vigil. This practice is often very popular with youth. Suggestions for holding a special Easter vigil are included in the Idea Pages of this section.

Our observances of Lent and its special days have evolved over the centuries. Christians in the first two centuries did not even commemorate Good Friday. They focused only on Easter Day. The first Christians met for worship on Holy Saturday around 6 p.m. They continued fasting, praying, and meditating through the night until about 3:00 a.m. on Easter Sunday. Then they celebrated the Eucharist. Many years later, fasting extended to include Friday. This period of 40 hours corresponds to the time Jesus' body lay in the tomb. Later still, the period of fasting extended to include all of Holy Week. By the year 600, the fast had extended to the 40 days (not including Sundays) prior to Easter. This time period reminds us of the 40 days Jesus spent in the wilderness preparing for public ministry. This became a time of final preparation for *catechumens* – those people who sought membership in the church by profession of faith and baptism. In time, many other church members undertook these 40 days of penitence and fasting for their own self-discipline. Reflecting on their own faith, these members joined with catechumens and renewed their baptismal promises at Easter.

Fasting has been practiced for centuries in connection with religious ceremonies. Fasts are observed among Christians, Jews, Muslims, Confucianists, Hindus, Taoists, Jainists, and adherents of other religious faiths. The early Christians associated fasting with penitence and purification (see Matthew 6:16; Luke 18:12). During the first two centuries, the Christian church established fasting as a voluntary preparation for receiving the sacraments of Holy Communion and Baptism and for the ordination of priests. Later, these fasts became obligatory, as did others subsequently added. After the Reformation, fasting was retained by most Protestant churches and was made optional in some cases. Stricter Protestants like the Puritans, however, condemned not only the festivals of the church, but its traditional fasts as well. The Orthodox Church today still observes fasts rigorously.

Fasting has been criticized from early times. Many Old Testament prophets and early Christian writers condemned the abuse of fasting as an empty formality by persons who led immoral lives. In modern times criticism of fasting has been based principally on other grounds. Physicians and psychologists have challenged the indiscriminate practice of rigorous fasting, maintaining that it is frequently harmful. In modern times the hunger strike, a form of fasting, has been employed as a political act of resistance. Innumerable political prisoners in various parts of the world have engaged in hunger strikes. Mahatma Gandhi, leader of the struggle for India's freedom, undertook fasts occasionally to compel his followers to obey his precept of nonviolence.

Implications for Youth Ministry

The introspective mood of this season suggests many possible themes for Lenten programs. Lent provides a unique opportunity to slow down, to look inside ourselves, and to reflect on our lives and our world. In the busy lives of many youth today, this can be a welcome invitation. So often they feel pressured by the world's preoccupation with outer appearances. Youth find it refreshing and affirming to take time examining their "inner selves."

Lent can help us reestablish a balance between God, self, and others. The story of Jesus' life is full of themes for youth reflection – facing difficult decisions, spiritual and religious experience, broken relationships. This may also be the time to discuss issues of faith and church membership with youth. The Idea Pages in this section provide suggestions for exploring these and other topics.

In many churches Lent is a time for fundraising for outreach projects, holding special gatherings, and preparing for the celebration of Easter. This may include planning special intergenerational services and events, preparing music and drama, or holding special study groups. These events provide opportunities for youth involvement in the life of the wider church community. With your clergy, try to plan ways that youth can organize, lead, and participate in the events of this season.

Today we are bombarded with messages about dieting from companies selling products with names like SlimFast and Fastin, meal replacement shakes, and juice fasts. Fasting is seen as a way to control weight. This can be a dangerous practice for young people. An alternative **Fasting and Feasting** reflection is included on page 84.

Labyrinths and Lent

Group Check-in

Ask everyone to position themselves according to their energy level. Think of the ceiling as the high energy mark and floor as the low energy mark. Group members might sit, lie on the floor, stand on a chair, etc. to express how they are feeling. Once everyone is in position, invite them to look around and notice where others have put themselves on the "energymeter." Does anyone want to share why they are feeling this way?

Significant Numbers

What numbers can you think of that have a special significance (e.g. "lucky 7," "sweet 16," "bad luck 13")? Brainstorm these and write down suggestions on a sheet of newsprint. Discuss their significance. What significant numbers do you know from the Bible? (e.g. seven days of Creation, the 50th "Jubilee" year, three days between death and resurrection, Jonah spent three days in the belly of a big fish) What Bible stories is the number 40 associated with? (e.g. Noah, Exodus, Jesus' temptation, Ascension) The number 40 signifies an important or special time. Why do you think the church began the tradition of observing a 40-day season of preparation (Season of Lent) before Easter?

Quiz

Try this fun quiz to introduce the Season of Lent.

You will need: copies of the **12 M in a Y Quiz** from page 83 and pencils

Give the youth a few minutes, individually or in pairs, to solve as many as possible. Share the answers and award a prize to the group that guessed the most correctly.

Answers: 1. Days in a Leap Year 2. Cards in a Deck 3. Months in a Year 4. Letters in the Alphabet 5. Holes on a Golf Course 6. Years in a Century 7. Wonders of the World 8. Books in the Old Testament 9. Days of Creation 10. Eggs in a Dozen 11. Days of Christmas 12. Weeks in a Year 13. Seasons in a Year 14. Minutes in an Hour 15. Days of Lent

Fasting and Feasting

Ash Wednesday marks the beginning of Lent. It is preceded by Shrove Tuesday, a time of preparation to enter the 40 days of the Season of Lent. The word "shrove" comes from the verb *to shrive*, which means to "confess and receive absolution (God's forgiveness)." On this night, it is traditional for Christians to use up the last of foods like eggs, sugar, and milk, to consume the last of the meat and other rich foods, in order to prepare to fast for the 40 days. Fasting is a tradition that has been practiced for centuries in connection with religious ceremonies. Today the original intent of fasting as a penitential discipline can be easily confused by messages about weight loss and dieting. Rather than fasting from food, which can be a hollow ritual, and even a dangerous one for young people, look at other behaviors and attitudes that you might "give up" for Lent. Hand out copies of **Fasting and Feasting** from page 84.

Pancakes and Ashes

Host a Shrove Tuesday Pancake Dinner. Combine ideas such as the **12M in a Y Quiz** and the **Fasting and Feasting** reflection to create a simple program to accompany the meal. (See *Youth Spirit*, Volume 1 for additional ideas.)

Walking a Labyrinth

Share information about the symbolism and history of labyrinths from **Sacred Pattern, Sacred Path** on page 85. If possible, find a labyrinth near you to walk using the Labyrinth Locator (see **Additional Resources**). Or create your own (see page 123 for instructions for making a masking tape labyrinth). Or use the **Finger Labyrinth** on page 86 as a substitute. Begin with the **Opening Up** meditation (see box).

Opening Up

Take your hands and squeeze them tight
So the whites of your knuckles can be seen
It may be sore
It may be intense
You may feel your nails dig in to your palms.

This is what God often encounters in us
Shut out
Closed tight
But slowly
Slowly
Slowly
Release your fists
As you allow the images and words in your mind
And all that they represent and symbolize –
Go.

Relax your fists
Those pains
Those hurts
And feel the blood running again
The pain releasing its grip
Uncurl your fingers
Slowly
Slowly
Feel them shake
Slowly
Uncurl and begin to straighten
So you see your palms
Red
Warm
And now
Slowly
Slowly
Open them fully
Open them to God
Open not just your hands but your hearts also
Open and ready to accept what God offers
Grace
Forgiveness
Healing
Freedom
Life
New life.

Adapted from a meditation by Rev. Roddy Hamilton,
Abbotsford Parish Church, Clydebank Scotland.
Used by permission.

Making a Finger Labyrinth

Give each person a copy of the
Finger Labyrinth from page 86.
Trace the outline of the labyrinth
with white glue and sprinkle with
sand. Shake off excess and allow to
dry. Invite youth to take the finger labyrinth
home and use it as a tool for meditation or
prayer.

Additional resources

Living the Labyrinth: 101 Paths to a Deeper Connection with the Sacred by Jill Kimberly Hartwell Geoffrion (Cleveland: Pilgrim Press, 2000)
Short, devotional meditations and suggestions for walking a labyrinth.
Praying the Labyrinth: A Journal for Spiritual Exploration by Jill Kimberly Hartwell Geoffrion (Cleveland: Pilgrim Press, 2000)
Full of spiritual exercises for self-discovery through scripture selections, journal questions, and poetry.
http://www.gracecathedral.org The website of Grace Cathedral in San Francisco includes a Labyrinth Locator, a searchable database of locations of labyrinths throughout North America, plus an online interactive labyrinth.

Closing Worship

Together create a worship center. Pour sand on
the surface of your worship table. Place a copy of
the **Finger Labyrinth** in the center. Invite each
group member in turn to trace the pattern of the
labyrinth with their finger, from the center back
out to the exit/entrance, and through the sand.
As each person traces their path out of the
labyrinth, invite the others to say:

We are all on the path
We are where we need to be
We journey where we need to go
For our hearts are restless until we find ourselves in God.

When the last person has finished, recite the
blessing:

Blessing:

Guide us, O God.
Walk with us.
Lift us when we stumble;
encourage us when we falter.
Bless us.
Amen.

The Season of Lent is 40 days long. Forty is a symbolic number in the Bible: Noah and his family spent 40 days and nights on the ark; the Hebrew people spent 40 years wandering in the desert before reaching the Promised Land; Jesus spent 40 days in the wilderness at the beginning of his earthly ministry. The number, according to scholars, simply indicates "a long time" and symbolizes wholeness. Guess the significance of the following numbers. The initials to the right of each number are the initials of what the number represents. Example: 365 D. in a Y. = 365 Days in a Year.

1. 366 D. in a L.Y.

2. 52 C. in a D.

3. 12 M. in a Y.

4. 26 L. in the A.

5. 18 H. on a G.C.

6. 100 Y. in a C.

7. 7 W. of the W.

8. 39 B. in the O.T.

9. 7 D. of C.

10. 12 E. in a D.

11. 12 D. of C.

12. 52 W. in a Y.

13. 4 S. in a Y.

14. 60 M. in an H.

15. 40 D. of L.

Fasting and Feasting

Fast from pessimism; feast on optimism.

Fast from criticism; feast on praise.

Fast from self-pity; feast on joy.

Fast from bitterness; feast on forgiveness.

Fast from idle gossip; feast on purposeful silence.

Fast from jealousy; feast on love.

Fast from discouragement; feast on hope.

Fast from complaining; feast on appreciation.

Fast from selfishness; feast on service.

Fast from fear; feast on faith.

Fast from anger; feast on patience.

Fast from self-concern; feast on compassion for others.

Fast from discontent; feast on gratitude.

For Lent this year I want to

fast from...

so I can feast on...

Sacred Pattern, Sacred Path

The word "labyrinth" refers to the maze-like patterns on the floors of some medieval churches. Used for centuries, the labyrinth is a contemplative tool for prayer, ritual, healing, and personal and spiritual growth. Unlike a maze, a labyrinth has only one path, which always leads to the center. One enters and returns on the same path. The labyrinth is based on the circle, the universal symbol for unity and wholeness. Its many turns reflect the cycles of nature and the journey of life that involves change and transition.

The Middle Ages showed a renewed interest in labyrinths and a design more complex than the classical seven-circuit labyrinth became popular. The most famous of these remaining labyrinths is at Chartres Cathedral near Paris, France. The labyrinth at Chartres was built around 1200 CE. Today, in our fast-paced technological society, we often have difficulty finding time for prayer and meditation. That is why some churches, such as Grace Cathedral in San Francisco, California, have rediscovered labyrinths. They have developed intricate pathways on floors within their church buildings and invite people to walk these paths in silence while reflecting on themselves as spiritual beings, created by God.

In the past labyrinths were walked as a pilgrimage or for repentance. When used for repentance the pilgrims would walk it on their knees. As a pilgrimage it was a questing, searching journey with the hope of becoming closer to God. Sometimes the eleven-circuit labyrinth would serve as a substitute for an actual pilgrimage to Jerusalem and as a result came to be called the "Chemin de Jerusalem" or Road of Jerusalem.

In walking the Chartres-style labyrinth, the walker meanders through each of the four *quadrants* several times before reaching the *center*. The path covers four directions, representing the four seasons and all of creation. At the center is a *rosette* design. In the mystical tradition the rose is a symbol for the Holy Spirit. The six petals represent the six days of creation and also represent the stages of planetary evolution (beginning with the left "petal"): mineral, vegetable, animal, human, angel, and unknown. The *labyrs* are the double-ax symbols visible at the turns, found between the turns throughout the labyrinth. When you look at the pattern as a whole from above, they form a cross. The *lunations* are the outer ring of partial circles that completes the outside circle of the labyrinth. There are 28½ lunations in each quadrant. It is thought that this was a lunar calendar that could be used to calculate the date of Easter.

As reaching the center is assured, walking the labyrinth is more about the journey than the destination. There are as many ways to walk the labyrinth as there are people who walk it. You can walk with or without your shoes on. (Although if it is a canvas model, you would most likely be asked to remove your shoes to keep the canvas clean.)

Before you begin, pause at the entry. Reflect on life. You may choose to kneel, bow, say a prayer, center yourself, whatever you choose, but walk with openness. If you wish, pose a question prior to entering, then completely relax your mind making no attempt to think about the question. Focus on the immediate experience – how you feel, how you are breathing, the pace and sound of your footsteps.

It is possible to have an uneventful experience, when nothing significant happens, the timing not right for anything to emerge. But you will still benefit from the walk, feeling more focused, more responsive to people. The first time you walk you will approach the experience like anything new (staying in your head). Once you know that you can't get lost and have a feel for it you will be quite at ease. Watching people walk can be a powerful meditation in itself.

If you are walking the labyrinth with others, make sure the person ahead of you has reached the first turn before you begin walking. As you walk, you will pass others on the path coming toward you, as everyone walks the same path in and out. Don't worry when you meet someone, you aren't going the wrong way.

Remember, a labyrinth is not a maze. It has no blind alleys, no wrong turns, and you cannot get lost in it. All you have to do is put one foot in front of the other and you will safely get to the center and back out again. A labyrinth is a right-brain task. It involves intuition, creativity, and imagery. With a maze many choices must be made and an active mind is needed to solve the problem of finding the center. With a labyrinth there is only one choice to be made. The choice is to enter or not.

Instructions: For Finger Labyrinth, enlarge on photocopier

Pilgrimage

Group Check-in

Invite group members to briefly share with a partner a memorable trip they have taken. Encourage partners to listen carefully and ask any questions for clarification after the person has finished speaking. When both people have had a chance to share, invite everyone to close their eyes and "take a picture" in their mind's eye, based on what their partner has described. Then take turns describing these "snap shots" to each other. For example, "I imagine your family standing in front of your van which is crammed with ski equipment and your brother is making a face at the back of your head because he is always bugging you. You are smiling and holding on to your new snowboard."

A History of Pilgrimage

A pilgrimage is a journey one takes in order to receive enlightenment, to experience a sense of deepening, to find wholeness. A pilgrimage is typically made to a place where a deity or saint was born, or accomplished great miracles, or to a site that features supernatural astrological or geographic qualities.

Some say pilgrimages began in earnest after the death of Jesus. Each city he visited during his lifetime was treasured by his followers, and after his death, those cities were visited in hopes of actually seeing his spirit manifestation, or in hopes of at least conjuring up vivid memories of him. Pilgrims in the Middle Ages set out on pilgrimages for a variety of reasons, mostly for spiritual blessing, but some went for monetary reasons, as the relics from sacred sites had great value in those days.

In fact the tradition of pilgrimage is found in every religion and began long before the death of Jesus. The ancient Egyptians journeyed to Sekhet's shrine at Bubastis or to Ammon's oracle at Thebes; the Greeks sought counsel from Apollo at Delphi and for cures from Asclepius at Epidaurus; the Mexicans gathered at the huge temple of Quetzalcoatl; the Inca massed in sun-worship at the famous Sun Temple in Cuzco; and the Bolivians at Lake Titicaca. Benares, now known as Varanasi, is an ancient pilgrimage site in India for Hindus. Perhaps the most noted pilgrimage tradition comes from the religion of Islam, which originated about 500 CE, and which requires all Moslems to visit the holy shrine of Kaaba, located in the Saudi Arabian city of Mecca, at least once during their lifetime.

In the early period of Hebrew history, pilgrimages were made to Shiloh and Dan (both in what is now Israel) and to Bethel (now in Jordan). In fact, it is said that Christian pilgrimage probably came from the Jewish practice of visiting the tombs of prophets and saints – the Jewish followers of Jesus knew him as a prophet and were practicing Jewish custom when, after his death, they visited his tomb or the places where he taught.

Reprinted from *Personal Pilgrimage* by Viki Hurst (Kelowna, BC: Northstone, 2000). Used by permission.

Plan a Pilgrimage

In her book *Personal Pilgrimage*, Viki Hurst outlines a simple process based on the four traditional phases of pilgrimage. The first phase she refers to as "heeding the call" – an awareness of the urge to venture forth which is characterized by a longing for deeper experiences than those immediately at hand. The second phase she calls "the night before" – a time to observe rituals that open the mind and prepare the heart for the sacred journey. The third phase is "the journey" itself. The fourth phase she calls "the homecoming" – a time to reflect on the experience as we re-enter daily life. This process can be adapted, or elements combined, to work in a shorter period of time. The key is to take time to prepare for the experience, and to allow time for silent and shared reflection immediately afterward. Choose four or five places of significance within easy distance of each other. Here are some suggestions:

- In most towns, there are churches within walking distance of each other. Although some are open during the day it would be wise to call ahead. You might ask if a church member could meet the group to talk for a few minutes about any special features of the sanctuary or about the church's history.

- Choose outdoor locations such as a cemetery, hilltop, park, botanic garden, or beach near you.

- Take a pilgrimage to places in your community such as a shelter for the homeless, detox center, food bank, or hospice. (See the idea for a **Walk of the Cross** on page 100.)

- When Jesus was 12, he went with his family to Jerusalem to celebrate the Passover. Arrange to visit a local synagogue to learn about the tradition of Passover and Jewish worship.

Ways you might prepare and/or reflect on the experience afterward

- Light a candle and focus on its flame. Use a simple prayer such as this Celtic Pilgrim's Prayer:

  Bless to us, O God
  The earth beneath our feet,
  Bless to us, O God,
  The path whereon we go,
  Bless to us, O God,
  The people whom we meet.

- Use the guided meditation **Opening Up** on page 82.

- Read a Bible passage related to the theme of your pilgrimage. You might reread the same passage at each stop and talk afterwards about new insights that were gained each time it was read.

- Choose a pilgrimage companion or inspirational guide whose life and words you would like to carry with you on your pilgrimage. *Personal Pilgrimage* (see **Additional Resources**) includes short biographies of well-known fellow pilgrims such as Moses, Mother Teresa, C.S. Lewis, Gandhi, and William Wordsworth.

- Have each person pack their own pilgrim's satchel with bottled water, a snack such as fruit or trail mix, a notebook and pencil, a Bible, and anything else you require for your particular pilgrimage (e.g. bus fare).

- Have each person write a postcard or letter describing the experience and what it meant to them. Mail these to participants during the week as a reminder of the experience.

- Begin and end the pilgrimage by walking a labyrinth. Pilgrims in the Middle Ages sometimes walked this on their knees as a sign of humility and penitence.

Making a Masking Tape Labyrinth

During the Middle Ages, walking a labyrinth was often the final stage of, or an alternative to, a traditional pilgrimage to Jerusalem. See **Sacred Pattern, Sacred Path** on page 85 for more information about labyrinths. If you would like to begin and end your pilgrimage by walking a labyrinth, follow the instructions for making a masking tape labyrinth on page 123 or use the **Finger Labyrinth** from page 86.

Additional resources

Personal Pilgrimage: One Day Soul Journeys for Busy People by Viki Hurst (Kelowna, BC: Northstone, 2000) Twelve templates for short, affordable, local versions of the traditional pilgrimage that rejuvenate, inspire, and enlighten.

http://www.sacredsites.com This website of anthropologist and photographer Martin Gray includes photographs of more than 1000 sacred sites in 70 countries.

Closing Worship

Together create a worship center. Include pictures of famous pilgrimage sites or symbols such as rocks, a Celtic cross, flowers. Pour sand on the surface of your worship table. Place a copy of the **Finger Labyrinth** in the center. Invite each group member in turn to trace the pattern of the labyrinth with their finger, from the center back out to the exit/entrance, and through the sand.

Invite group members to add to the list of pilgrimage sites the names of places that are sacred to them (e.g. summer camp, park, grandparent's house). Read the list slowly, pausing briefly after each is named to allow for reflection. Conclude with a prayer: Stonehenge, the Great Pyramids of Egypt, Machu Pichu, Chichen Itza, Tikal, Mount Fuji, Bethlehem, Jerusalem, Cave of Quarantana, Mount Sinai, Mecca, Bodh Gaya site of Buddha's enlightenment, Iona, Lourdes, Chartres, Canterbury, the Berlin Wall, the Vietnam Memorial in Washington, the National Peacekeeping Monument in Ottawa, (add others).

Prayer:

Blessed is the spot, and the house,
and the place, and the city,
and the heart, and the mountain,
and the refuge, and the cave,
and the valley, and the land,
and the sea, and the island,
and the meadow
where mention of God has been made,
and God's praise glorified.

– Baha'i prayer by Baha'u'llah

The Bible

Group Check-in

Have everyone name a favorite Bible story or character from the Bible and explain why it is their favorite.

Storytelling

Provide paper and pens. Invite the youth to write the details they remember of a familiar fairy tale such as Little Red Riding Hood or Cinderella. Have group members read what they have written aloud, in turn. What differences do you notice between the various versions? How do you account for these differences? Alternately, use **The Christmas Quiz** on page 119 to explore the well-known story of Jesus' birth as recorded in the Gospels of Matthew and Luke. Share reactions to the answers on page 120. What other sources have influenced our knowledge of the details of this story? (e.g. greeting cards that show Mary riding a donkey, children's storybooks that show the Magi arriving at the manger)

Then compare passages from the Bible that tell the same story, with slight variations, such as Genesis 1:1–2:4a with Genesis 2:4b–22, or Genesis 12:10–20 with Genesis 20:1–3, 6–18. How do you feel about these different versions? Share the information from the box **The Pentateuch** on this page.

The Pentateuch

The first five books of the Bible are called the *Pentateuch* (Greek for "five scrolls"). In the 18th and 19th centuries, scholars began to study differences in the style and language within these books. They noticed that the same story was often repeated with slight variances. For example, sometimes names had slightly different spellings, such as Sarah/Abraham and Sarai/Abram. They suggested that these differences indicated seams where new material had been inserted or where different versions of one story were combined. Because of these inconsistencies, scholars believe that at least four writers or groups of writers compiled and edited sacred stories, over many years, into a cohesive narrative – what we now know as the books of Genesis, Exodus, Leviticus, Deuteronomy, and Numbers.

Bible Belief Cards

Copy and cut apart the **Bible Belief Cards** on page 91. Prepare a set for each youth and place these in an envelope. Hand out envelopes to youth and have them read each statement carefully, separating these into two piles: one for statements they believe about the Bible and another for statements they do not believe. When they are finished, have them find a partner and share their belief statements. Ask each pair to choose one statement that they both agree on (one that they do believe or that they don't believe) and discuss this. Then invite them to present their ideas to the rest of the group.

Afterwards discuss:

- Why is the Bible an important part of Christian religion?
- How does the Bible help you with daily situations you face?
- What questions do you have about the Bible?

What the Bible Says About…

William Shakespeare said, "Even the devil can cite scripture for his own purpose." What do you think he meant by this? Have you ever had an argument with someone about what the Bible says, or about how to interpret what the Bible says? Why do you think Christians don't always have the same understanding of what the Bible says? Some Christians believe the Bible is the infallible word of God. Others believe it is important to consider the context – the time in history and the circumstances – it was written in, as well as our own experience and tradition, and to use our own reason to understand what the passage means for Christians today. Some Christians view the Bible as "literally true," while others view the Bible as "containing truth."

What controversial issues do Christians sometimes argue about? List suggestions on newsprint. Decide as a group to explore one or more of these topics in more depth. A book like *The Bible Tells Me So* (see **Additional Resources**) will provide some useful background and context to the original meaning of these passages and differing views among Christians today. Or discuss the article **Spare the Rod, Spoil the Child** on page 92.

Scripture Cake

To make this delicious recipe youth use their Bibles to figure out the ingredients. This recipe works best using the *New International Version* or the *New Revised Standard Version* of the Bible.

To make Scripture Cake you will need:

1 1/2 cups (375 mL)	Jeremiah 6:20
2 cups (500 mL)	Psalm 55:21a
6	Job 39:14
3 Tbsp. (45 mL)	1 Samuel 14:25
1/2 cup (125 mL)	Judges 4:19a
4 1/2 cups (1125 mL)	1 Kings 4:22
1 tsp. (5 mL)	Leviticus 2:13
2 tsp. (10 mL)	Amos 4:5
1 1/2 tsp. (7.5 mL)	2 Chronicles 9:9
2 cups (500 mL)	Numbers 17:8, chopped
4 cups (1000 mL)	1 Samuel 30:12 (2 cups of each)

Instructions: Some interpretation is needed: Jeremiah reference to "cane" or "calamus" will mean sugar; Amos reference to "leavened" bread will mean baking powder; for the 2 Chronicles reference to "spices" use 1/2 tsp. each of cinnamon, nutmeg, and cloves. Grease four small loaf pans. Mix ingredients, in the order given, in a large bowl. Beat thoroughly. Bake for 2 1/2 hours at 250° F (160°C). *Can also be baked as cupcakes, for 20 minutes at 350° F (180° C).*

Bible Tag

In this game the leader yells out a Bible verse and the goal of the players is to see who can find it the fastest. It's fun and it can help youth learn how to find their way around in the Bible.

Take some time as you explain how the game is played, to describe the structure of the Bible and how it is organized.

You will need: Bibles

Instructions: One person begins by yelling out a passage. The first player who finds the passage is the winner, but you must wait until everyone has found it before reading it. The first person who found the passage gets to yell out another Bible verse, and so on. The first time you play, if your group is particularly inexperienced, they may yell out things like "Psalm 190" or "Obadiah 12:93" and you have to stop and explain to them that they should pick verses that really exist, by flipping through the Bible and choosing something that catches their eye. Players can use the Table of Contents at the front of their Bible to locate a book.

Additional resources

The Bible Tells Me So: Uses and Abuses of Holy Scripture by Jim Hill and Rand Cheadle (New York: Anchor Books, 1996)
This book describes how preachers, politicians, and others have selectively used the Bible to reach often contradictory conclusions on issues such as women's rights, abortion, capital punishment, slavery, homosexuality – even appropriate hairstyles.
The Story of the Bible: How the World's Bestselling Book Came to Be (Kelowna, BC: Wood Lake Books, 1998)
Youth will enjoy discovering the long line of faithful people who have remembered, written down, compiled, edited, copied, and translated, so that we might have the Bible as we know it today. A great resource for confirmation classes, retreats, or midweek programs.
Cracking the Cover: A Beginner's Guide to the Bible by Ross L. Smillie (Toronto: UCPH, 1997)
A well-written introduction to the Bible for youth groups and adult Bible study. Includes useful exercises for reflection in a workbook-style format.
http://www.religioustolerance.org This website includes thought-provoking essays on what the Bible says about suicide, the death penalty, human cloning.

Closing Worship

Prayer:
O God,
help us in our study of your Word,
not only to know about you,
but also to know you;
not only to learn about you,
but to encounter you;
not only to grow in knowledge,
but also to increase in understanding.
Amen.

Bible Belief Cards

The Bible is a guidebook to learn the will of God.	The Bible is the Word of God; the people who wrote it were given the words to write by God.
The Bible gives guidelines for living the Christian life.	God gave biblical writers the basic ideas or inspiration, and they used their own lives and experience to write the Bible.
God is revealed through the events of the Bible.	The Bible is one of many sacred books. It is no more or less important than the Koran is to Muslims or the Talmud is to Jewish people.
The Bible is absolutely true and completely accurate.	What the Bible says doesn't really relate to our lives today in the 21st century.
The Bible predicts the end of the world.	What the Bible says does relate to our lives today in the 21st century.
The Bible must be interpreted; there is more to scripture than what appears at face value.	Reading the Bible can help me in my life.

Spare the Rod, Spoil the Child

In July 2001, seven children were taken into protective custody by Ontario's Family and Child Services on suspicion that they were being physically abused by their parents. After reviewing the case, an Ontario judge handed down his decision that the children, ages six to 14, could return to live with their mother and father again, on the condition that the parents refrain from spanking or hitting the children – at least for the time being.

The case emphasizes the delicate balance between legitimate concerns of the state and the legitimate private rights of citizens to freedom of religious expression. The mother and father belong to the Church of God and have insisted that the Bible gives them the right to spank their children.

The Criminal Code of Canada permits parents to spank their children, as a form of discipline, as long as they use "reasonable force."

Rev. Henry Hildebrandt, the minister of the church the family attends, argued that corporal punishment is endorsed by the Bible, which warns against sparing the rod. "(Spanking) has to be part of bringing up children," Hildebrandt said. "It has to be done in a loving, in a kind way. But it has to be done, nevertheless." He said the parents used a strap on their children only when other methods of discipline failed.

Last year, Family and Children Services investigated 71,000 allegations of child abuse, seizing 14,000 children. Although it would not comment directly on the Aylmer case because it's now before the courts, Family and Children Services said removing youngsters from a home is considered a drastic step, taken only when authorities believe children are in danger.

What does the Bible say?
Below is a list of scripture references to read and discuss

Proverbs 13:24
Proverbs 22:15
Proverbs 23:13–14
Matthew 19:13–15
Colossians 3:21

Questions for discussion:

• What assumptions do these passages from the Bible make about the nature of children/people, about the rights and responsibilities of parents, and the result of physical punishment? Do you agree?

• Some people believe school discipline is a problem that has only become worse since laws have been strengthened to prevent school authorities from using physical punishment to discipline students. Do you agree? Do you think physical punishment is justified in some cases?

• Some people advocate a return to corporal punishment and school prayer as a way to return order and teach respect for authority. Do you agree? Why is it important to have respect for authority? How do you think people learn to respect/disrespect people in authority?

• Do you agree with Rev. Hildebrandt that there is a "loving, kind way" to use physical force to discipline children?

Balance

Group Check-in

Have group members stand in a circle. One at a time, have them make a gesture or physical movement that symbolizes how they are feeling at the moment. All together, the other members of the group then echo the movement back to them.

Life Wheel Exercise

Hand out copies of **The Life Wheel** from page 96 and allow time for the youth to complete these and read the descriptions at the bottom of the page. Reflect with a partner: What are some activities you like to do, or need to do more regularly, to bring more balance and wholeness to your day?

A Parable about Balance

You will need: a large glass bowl (e.g. punch bowl), 12 rocks about the size of your fist, very coarse gravel or pebbles, sand, water

Instructions: Set out the bowl and large rocks. Keep the other items hidden from view. Inform the group that you are going to do a little experiment. Begin by carefully placing as many of the large rocks in the glass bowl as will fit. When the bowl is filled to the top, ask "Is the bowl full?" (They will likely say yes, but some may realize more can fit in the bowl.) Bring out the gravel and dump some over the rocks, shaking the bowl to cause pieces of the gravel to work themselves down into the spaces between the larger rocks. Ask the group if they think the bowl is full now. (They will probably have caught on now and suggest more can fit.) Bring out the sand and dump some in the bowl so that it goes into the spaces left between the rocks and the gravel. Then bring out the water and pour it in until the bowl is filled to the brim. Ask if they think the bowl is full now. (Most will say yes, although some of the chemistry students in the group will recognize that many other substances such as salt, sugar, and other things that will *dissolve* in water could also be added and likely not cause the bowl to overflow.)

Jesus used stories, called *parables*, to teach people "spiritual truths" – parables such as the Lost Coin, the Lost Sheep, the Prodigal Son, and the Good Samaritan. He often used objects and situations that would have been common and familiar to his audience – like this bowl, and these rocks, and this

water. If Jesus were to use this parable, what do you think he might be trying to teach us? (e.g. remember to put the big rocks in first or you'll never get them in at all; don't sweat the little stuff – the gravel, the sand – or you won't have time for the big, important stuff.) Affirm all of their suggestions.

Spiritual Practice

Lent is 40 days (not counting the six Sundays) from Ash Wednesday to Holy Saturday. In the Bible, the number 40 is often used to represent "significant time." In the gospels we are told that Jesus spent "40 days" in the wilderness, fasting and being tempted. Lent is a symbolic journey toward Easter, 40 days that encourage us to look inward, to pause and take time to reflect, to examine our lives. Jesus knew the importance of taking time to do this. There are many stories recorded in the gospels that tell of times when Jesus went off by himself, to think and to pray, though the pressures of his growing popularity with the crowds made this nearly impossible.

Likewise, it is hard for most of us, with the pace of life we lead, to find time and space to slow down, to be quiet and listen for God's voice. The message of Lent is just what so many of us in our consumer-driven, workaholic society need to hear: that many of life's blessings can only be found through letting go of striving and accumulating. Lent invites us to practice "intentional spirituality," to find time for the care and feeding of our souls.

Divide into small groups and give each a passage to read and reflect on. They might prepare to act out the passage for the other groups. Suggested passages: Matthew 14:1–13a (Jesus grieves the death of John), Matthew 14:22–23b (Jesus prays on a mountainside), Mark 1:29–39 (Jesus escapes the crowds), Mark 4:35–41 (Jesus in the boat with his disciples), Mark 10:13–16 (Jesus and the children), Mark 14:1–11 (Jesus anointed at Bethany), Mark

14:32–42 (Jesus prays at Gethsemane), Luke 4:12–16a (Jesus goes to the synagogue), Luke 6:12–16 (Jesus prays and chooses helpers).

Afterwards discuss:

• What is happening in this passage?

• What "life-balance" is Jesus modeling?

• Where would/do you go when you need time to yourself?

Guest Speaker

In the West there is a growing interest and acceptance of Eastern philosophy and practices such as acupuncture, Tai Chi, meditation, and yoga. Some have pursued this as a spiritual path; others have adopted practices in order to relieve stress, cope with physical pain, or bring more balance into their lives. There has also been a resurgence of interest among Christians in ancient practices such as prayer, healing, pilgrimage, and labyrinths. Invite someone who practices a life-balancing technique such as yoga, meditation, Tai Chi, or centering prayer to visit the group. If it is appropriate, have your guest lead the youth through some basic moves and talk a bit about how they got into it and how it benefits them. Why not introduce the youth to several of these? Plan to have a different guest each week for four weeks. At the end of the four weeks, take time to reflect on the experience. Which was most interesting? Could you imagine incorporating one of these techniques into your life? Did you notice any changes in your body after each exercise?

How God Works in My Life

Write the list of statements below on a sheet of newsprint. Hand out pieces of paper. Have the youth fold their paper in thirds so that when unfolded they have three columns. Label one column "Primarily My Responsibility," the second column "Primarily God's Responsibility," and the third column "Too Close to Call." Ask them to read over the list of statements you've recorded on newsprint and place a check mark in the column according to whether they think this is primarily their responsibility, primarily God's, or a combination. Afterward, compare answers with a partner and discuss your reasons. How do you think God performs those functions that you feel God is responsible for?

1. Making the decision whether I marry or remain single.

2. Protecting me from drunken drivers.

3. Whether I have faith in God/Jesus.

4. Keeping me in good health.

5. Choosing my career/vocation.

6. Understanding the Bible.

7. Peace in the world.

8. Whether I succeed in my goals.

9. Developing my gifts and talents.

10. Whether I will be baptized/ confirmed.

– Adapted from an exercise in *Get'Em Talking: 104 Great Discussion Starters for Youth Groups* by Mike Yaconelli and Scott Koenigsaecker (Grand Rapids: Zondervan, 1989).

Closing Worship

Invite everyone to get into a comfortable position and close their eyes. Have a volunteer read the meditation **Footprints in the Sand** on the next page.

FOOTPRINTS IN THE SAND

(Based on the original poem "Footprints" by Margaret Fishback Powers.)

Imagine you and the Lord Jesus are walking along the beach together. For much of the way the Lord's footprints go along steadily, consistently, rarely varying in the pace. But your prints are in a disorganized stream of zigzags, starts, stops, turnarounds, circles, departures, and returns. For much of the way it seems to go like this. But gradually, your footprints come in line with the Lord's, soon paralleling his consistently. You and Jesus are walking as true friends.

This seems perfect, but then an interesting thing happens; your footprints that once etched the sand next to his are now walking precisely in his steps. Inside his large footprints is the smaller "sandprint," safely enclosed. You and Jesus are becoming one; this goes on for many miles.

But gradually you notice another change. The footprints inside the larger footprints seem to grow larger. Eventually they disappear altogether. There is only one set of footprints. They have become one; again this goes on for a long time.

But then something awful happens. The second set of footprints is back. This time it seems even worse than before. Zigzags all over the place. Stop...start. Deep gashes in the sand. A real mess of prints. You're amazed and shocked. So you ask: "Lord, I understand the first scene with the zigzags, fits, starts, and so on. I was a new Christian, just learning. But you walked on through the storm and helped me learn to walk with you."

"That is correct," Jesus replies.

"Then, when the smaller footprints were inside of yours, I was actually learning to walk in your steps. I followed you very closely."

"Very good. You have understood everything so far."

"Then the smaller footprints grew and eventually filled in with yours. I suppose that I was actually growing so much that I was becoming more like you in every way."

"Precisely."

"But this is my question, Lord. Was there a regression or something? The footprints went back to two, and this time it was worse than the first."

The Lord smiles, then laughs. "You didn't know?" he says. "That was when we danced."

- Source: the Internet

Life Wheel

Look at the pie shapes below and read the categories. Take a minute to think about how much time and energy you spend on these areas of your life. Place a small dot in the pie wedge indicating how much. The center of the pie represents very little. The further you place the dot from the center represents more time/energy. For example, if you spent very little time doing physical activity and a lot of time studying, these wedges might look like this (see illustration). When you have done this for all seven categories, draw a line connecting the dots. What shape emerges?

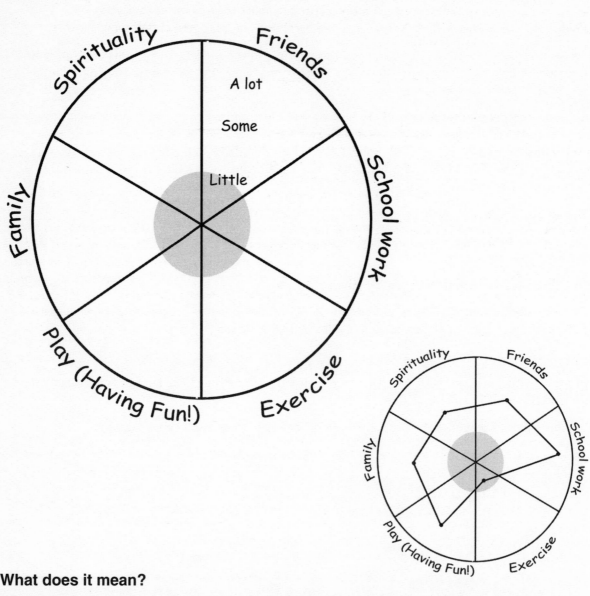

What does it mean?

If it looks like a flat tire... Many of us suffer from the "flat tire syndrome." While many aspects of our lives may be balanced, there is often one area that is less developed. Think about ways you can develop this area of your life.

If it looks like a star or triangle... Are there several areas of life that may be out of balance? Choose one that you would like to work on for the next week, month, or year. What are some of the ways you could help bring this area of life more into balance with the others?

If it looks like a circle... You must work hard at keeping your life in balance. Keep up the good work! Sometimes changes in our lives can cause us to neglect an area for a time. Try this exercise again in six months to see if you are keeping the balance.

Section E:

Mood and Flavor of the Season

Easter is the oldest festival of the church and the focal point of the Christian Year. The early church celebrated Easter long before observing the Seasons of Lent or Christmas. The Season of Easter, or the "Great 50 Days," begins on Easter Sunday and continues until Pentecost, 50 days later. The Sundays of this season are called the Sundays of Easter. The liturgical colors of white and gold reflect the joy of this season.

During the Season of Easter we read stories of Jesus' appearances to the disciples after the Resurrection. As the disciples experienced Jesus with them in various places, the good news of Easter gradually dawned on them. We also read stories from the Book of Acts about the church's beginning and the spread of the Christian faith. Throughout this season we balance the disciples' gradual and growing awareness in the gospels with the disciples' bold words and actions following Pentecost.

Special Days

Forty days after Easter Sunday Jesus ascended into heaven. We normally celebrate this on the Sunday nearest to Ascension Day. On Earth Day or Rogation Sunday, many congregations focus on concern for the environment. Rogation Sunday is normally celebrated on the Sunday preceding Ascension Day. The name comes from the Latin *rogare* meaning "to beg" or "to ask." Traditionally, it was a special time of prayer for and blessing of the spring crops. The English emphasized seed time, planting, and prayers for a bountiful harvest. Open-air services, processions through the fields and farms, and "beating the bounds" or walking the boundaries of the parish marked the observance.

Although not part of the Christian Year, many churches celebrate the second Sunday in May as Christian Family Sunday, the day secular society calls Mother's Day. On this day many denominations emphasize living in harmony – not only with our parents and siblings, but also with all God's children who are our brothers and sisters.

The day of Pentecost, the last Sunday of the Easter Season, is a festival of fire and wind and the Holy Spirit. Vivid red, the liturgical color for this day, signifies the tongues of fire that rested on each disciple. The fire transformed the followers of Jesus (disciples) into the bearers of the message (apostles), who were "sent forth." Red is also the color of martyrdom, reminding us how many of the early Christians were put to death for their beliefs.

On the day of Pentecost we celebrate not only the Holy Spirit poured out on the disciples, but also God's Spirit at work today and the gifts of the Spirit in each of us.

Pentecost existed before the early church. Fifty days after the Jewish festival of Passover came the spring harvest festival of Pentecost, or the "Feast of Weeks." Greek-speaking Jews named the festival using the Greek word *Pentecost,* meaning "50th." This celebration marked the end of the grain harvest and the beginning of the season of first fruits. In May, farmers harvested the wheat planted in November. Before the people ate any of the newly harvested crop, they dedicated it to God. Each family made two loaves from the new wheat, baked the bread according to laws (found in the Book of Leviticus), and presented it as an offering at the temple. Today Jewish people usually refer to the Feast of Weeks as *Shavuot.* At this Jewish festival Jewish boys and girls are confirmed (*bar mitzvah* and *bat mitzvah*). For Christians, Pentecost is also a time for baptism, as described in Acts, and for confirmation – the affirmation of baptismal faith.

Implications for Youth Ministry

Every year on the second Sunday of Easter, the lectionary reading includes the story of "doubting Thomas" – the disciple who was absent when Jesus first appeared to the disciples in the upper room. Thomas refused to believe that Christ had risen until he had seen him for himself (John 20:24–29). This story can be very meaningful for adolescents who engage in similar questioning about their beliefs and values. Use this story as a discussion starter about the questions and doubts of the youth in the group. Youth might enjoy interviewing some older members of the congregation and asking them about their beliefs, questions, and doubts.

The focus on the spread of the Christian faith and on the beginning of the early church with the apostles provides many possibilities for youth groups. Does the group want to plan a retreat? Use this as an opportunity to reflect on experiences of early Christians who lived in community. What does it mean to be a Christian today? The Idea Pages in this section include the suggestion to visit churches of other denominations to experience the variety and diversity within the Christian tradition.

The environment and community are also important themes for youth. The Idea Pages in this section include resources for exploring the Jubilee theme of "renewal of the earth." The youth may want to participate in special Earth Day observances or lead an intergenerational service focused on concern for the environment.

At this time of year they look back on the past year, and they may look forward to personal plans that will scatter them out into the world, like the apostles scattered after Pentecost. If the youth do not meet during the summer, plan how you will bring closure to the group. Gather and share information on summer services, leadership training, or camping opportunities for youth. Ideas for retreats and wind-up activities are also included in this section.

Easter Vigil

A History of Vigils

There are two traditional times during Holy Week to observe a vigil. The scriptures record that Jesus died at about 3:00 p.m. on Friday afternoon. Because Jewish laws did not allow work to be done on the Sabbath, which begins at sundown on Friday, the disciples were unable to prepare his body for burial. So early vigils may have commemorated the vigil they kept, as they waited for daybreak on Sunday (the end of the Sabbath). This type of vigil lasts roughly 40 hours, corresponding with the time Jesus' body lay in the grave. When the women arrived with spices to anoint the body, they found the tomb empty.

It is also traditional to hold a vigil on the evening of Maundy Thursday, when we recall the story of how Jesus asked his disciples to stay awake with him while he prayed in the Garden of Gethsemane and they could not. This shorter vigil, which might last a few hours or through the night, offers a time to reflect on the ways we have not done what God has asked of us, times when we have denied Jesus by our words or actions.

40-Hour Vigil

If you are holding a 40-hour vigil, plan a variety of activities, some active and some reflective. Incorporate the suggestions below with your own ideas.

- Plan an old-fashioned egg hunt, or see the idea for an Egg Hunt (below). Also see page 160 of *Youth Spirit* (Volume 1) for game ideas involving Easter eggs.
- Bake bread for Communion on Easter Sunday.
- Invite someone from a local Amnesty International group to talk about people who are imprisoned, as Jesus was, for their religious or political beliefs. Write letters on behalf of prisoners of conscience.
- Watch a movie such as *Jesus Christ Superstar*, *Jesus of Nazareth*, or a children's classic, such as *The Lion, The Witch and the Wardrobe*. You might watch two different ones and compare the depiction of the same character in each.
- Create Easter banners to decorate the sanctuary.
- (See next page for information on the paschal candle.) Light the new paschal candle at dawn and process into the darkened sanctuary. Individual candles may be lit from it to spread light to all the sanctuary. **Prayer for Easter Sunrise:** May the Morning Star which never sets find this flame still burning: Christ, that Morning Star, who came back from the dead to shed light on all humankind, your Son who lives and reigns for ever and ever. Amen.

Jesus Christ Superstar

When *Jesus Christ Superstar* made its Broadway debut almost three decades ago, it was attacked by everyone from evangelist Billy Graham to the Jewish Anti-Defamation League. Protested as a blasphemous, "hippie" version of the gospel that emphasized the humanity of Jesus rather than his divinity, many other people credit the musical as having revived their faith by offering them a contemporary and powerful perspective on the person of Jesus of Nazareth. One of the most controversial things about this rock opera, written by Andrew Lloyd Webber and Tim Rice, is that it doesn't include a resurrection scene. Would it make a difference if Jesus had never risen from the dead? To find out more about the movie based on the Broadway revival in 2000 visit http://www.jcs.pair.com. It is available on video and DVD and could be incorporated into your vigil. Highly recommended.

Easter Banners

Here's an idea from Abbotsford Parish Church, in Scotland, for an easy, disposable banner.

You will need: banner paper/newsprint, colored crepe paper, glue or stapler, gold ribbon

Instructions: Cut strips of banner paper/newsprint 6 feet (2 m) or longer, depending on the height of the walls you will hang these on. Cut pieces of dark blue, light blue, green, yellow, orange, pink, and red crepe paper streamers. Glue one end of strips or staple these to the newsprint – progressing from top to bottom in order from dark blue to red. Weave in gold ribbon.

About 25 feet tall, these banners represent hope and resurrection through the gold ribbons strung through the rainbows.

Photo from Roddy Hamilton

The Paschal Candle

This is the largest candle ever used by the church. Usually it has a Greek cross inscribed on it; into the corners created by the intersection of the arms of the cross are inscribed the four numerals of the Year of Our Lord (the calendar year) in which the candle is lighted. Above and below the cross are the first and last letters of the Greek alphabet, the Alpha and Omega, signifying God who is "the beginning and the end." The paschal candle reminds us of the pillar of fire that Moses and the Hebrew people followed by night as they journeyed in the wilderness to the Promised Land. It is customary for churches to introduce a new paschal candle at Easter.

Maundy Thursday Vigil

If this will be a true "vigil," plan a variety of activities to keep the youth active and awake. Incorporate the suggestions below with your own ideas.

- Share a meal together, remembering Jesus' last supper with his friends on the eve of the Passover. Sample the foods from the Seder, the traditional Passover meal eaten by Jews. See page 136 of *Youth Spirit* (Volume 1) for instructions for preparing a Seder Meal. See the outline on page 102 for a **Maundy Thursday Tenebrae** to use at the conclusion of the meal.

- Invite the youth to bring 30 pieces of silver (nickels, dimes, quarters). As they arrive, provide cloth circles (diameter: 4 in/10 cm) and string. Place coins in the center of the fabric, gather up sides, and tie with string to create a coin bag. See the **Litany of Confession and Assurance of Pardon** on page 101.

- If your church observes the tradition of reserving the sacrament (bread and wine) for Good Friday, set aside a place in the sanctuary (perhaps a small chapel) to symbolize the Garden of Gethsemane. Fill it with plants and candles. Divide the youth into vigil groups (or pairs) to take turns in 20-minute segments throughout the night keeping watch with Jesus. During these times, short readings are interspersed with silence. While the smaller groups are taking turns keeping watch, the larger group might play games, sing, and do other activities.

- Share Communion/Eucharist together. See the **Liturgy for Communion** on page 102.

- See the **Rock Meditation** on page 101 for instructions on leading a meditation on the last hours of Jesus' life.

The Road to Jerusalem

In the Middle Ages, labyrinths sometimes served as a substitute for an actual pilgrimage to Jerusalem and as a result came to be called the *Chemin de Jerusalem*, or "Road of Jerusalem." Use ideas on page 88 to create your own labyrinth. There are many ways to walk the labyrinth. Instead of walking the pathway to the center and back out, walk the cross. Begin at the entrance, walking straight across the entire labyrinth to the far side of it. Then walk back to the center. Next, walk out and back one of the "arms," returning to the center. Then walk out and back the other arm, returning once again to the center. In the 11-circuit labyrinth this means walking on the *labyrs*, the double-ax symbols visible at the turns. If you were to look at a labyrinth from above, the *labyrs* form the pattern of a large cross.

Good Friday Walk of the Cross

(See box for information on the *Via Dolorosa*.) Host a "Walk of the Cross" in your community. Plan a route that will include social service agencies and organizations that work with families, people on income assistance, the homeless, unemployed, and marginalized. At each stop offer prayers for the people who work and volunteer their time, and for the people the organization serves. You might ask someone from the agency to speak briefly about the work it does. Begin with a prayer or simple liturgy such as the one included on the **Worship Resources for Easter Vigils** page.

Via Dolorosa

The term *Via Dolorosa* (The Way of Sorrows) was popularized in the 16th century and its 14 stations were standardized by the Franciscans during the 19th century. This route, followed by the world's orthodox Christians, led from the Antonia Fortress, where Jesus appeared before Pilate and was condemned, out to Calvary (called *Golgotha* in Greek), which was outside the city walls at that time.

Rock Meditation

This meditation uses rocks to reflect on the last days of Jesus' life.

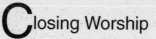

You will need: a Bible, rocks of various sizes and shapes, and copies of **The Stones Shout Out** on pages 103–104.

Have everyone choose a rock. Invite them to examine it in silence and become familiar with it. Think about how the rock feels in your hand. How does it fit in your palm? Are there any lines, designs, or colors that are unusual? What is the shape of your rock? The texture? Is it smooth or rough? Are there any sharp edges? These rocks will be part of our meditation. At the end of each section, the two "Readers" will place their rocks in the center, piling them on top of each other to create an altar, or *cairn*. A cairn is a pile of stones heaped up as memorial, tomb, or landmark. Any remaining rocks can be piled on the cairn at the end.

Additional resources

Kneeling in Jerusalem, by Ann Weems (Louisville: Westminster/John Knox Press, 1992)
A collection of poems that reflect on the journey through Lent to Easter.
The Courage for Hallelujahs: Alternate Worship Resources for Lent and Easter, edited by Keri Wehlander (Toronto: United Church Publishing House, 1997)

Egg Hunt

Purchase plastic eggs that can be opened. Place symbols of the passion story inside (e.g. a small rock, a tissue, a nail, a silver coin, a piece of bread, spices/whole cloves). After they are hidden, have the youth hunt for the eggs. When they have found them all, gather in a circle and open the eggs. Place the objects on a low table. Invite group members to pick up an object and use these to tell parts of the "story" of Holy Week in their own words. Don't worry if the story doesn't unfold chronologically. Objects may symbolize more than one thing. For example, the tissue might symbolize the tears that the women shed at the foot of the cross or the sheet they wrapped Jesus' body in.

Closing Worship

Read the story **Philip's Easter Egg** from page 105.

Prayer for Easter Morning:

O God, we give thanks for your son Jesus who was fully human –
who lived and knew friendship, love, pain, and sorrow,
and who died but rose again.
We give you thanks for words of comfort in times of difficulty and grief,
for the gift and mystery of life,
and for the reassurance of our life with you after death. Amen.

Litany of Confession and Assurance of Pardon

Reader 1: Associating with Jesus and following his cause was often costly for the disciples. They risked losing friends, family, and even their lives. Sometimes they acted courageously. They cheered for Jesus, even when they were cautioned to keep silent. At other times they lost their courage, leaving Jesus to suffer alone.

Reader 2: Sometimes we have a difficult time following Jesus. We fail to stand up for what we believe. We don't protest against injustice. We let others suffer alone, when they need our support. Yet we are still invited to start again.

Reader 1: As you hold your bag of coins, think about how Jesus must have felt on the night he was arrested. Think of the times when, like Jesus' first disciples, you have been silent when you should have spoken. *(Allow time for silent reflection.)* Think of times when, like Judas, you have acted or spoken in ways that have been hurtful or betrayed another's trust. *(Allow time for silent reflection.)* Place these regrets before God, knowing that we are forgiven and can begin again. *(Invite participants to place their bag of 30 silver coins on an offering plate.)*

Reader 2: Now think of those times when you have put your faith into action as Jesus and his followers did. Imagine also, the ways that you will follow Jesus in the future. *(Allow time for silent reflection.)* These special times remind us that we can live faithful lives, even if we have made mistakes in the past. God is with us, strengthening us to live in love and courage. Thanks be to God!

Worship Resources for Easter Vigils

Maundy Thursday Tenebrae

Drape long pieces of fabric on the floor in the shape of a cross. Place six votive candles in glass jars and one white Christ candle on the fabric. Light the candles. Read the first line of the Tenebrae, extinguish a candle, and pass the snuffer to the person next to you to extinguish the next candle.

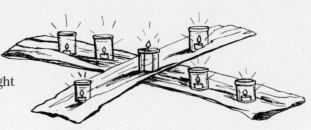

This is the night when, after his Last Supper with Jesus, Judas met with the authorities to plan the arrest of Jesus. *(One candle is extinguished.)* This is the night when all the disciples would leave Jesus alone to suffer! *(A second candle is extinguished.)* This is the night when even Peter, the most enthusiastic disciple, the one who promised to always stay by Jesus, would deny he knew Jesus. *(A third candle is extinguished.)* This is the night, in the Garden of Gethsemane, when Jesus prayed that he wouldn't have to go through with the suffering and death to come. *(A fourth candle is extinguished.)* This is the night Jesus prayed that God's will, not his own, be done. And while he struggled, his friends slept. *(A fifth candle is extinguished.)* This is the night when Judas arrived with the authorities and betrayed Jesus with a kiss on the cheek. Then the soldiers seized Jesus and led him away – alone. *(The sixth candle is extinguished. The white Christ candle now burns alone.)*

Prayer for Maundy Thursday: Loving God, as we remember the last few hours of Jesus life, help us to keep vigil with you so that we might be witnesses, as the first disciples were, to the good news of Easter. Amen.

Liturgy for Communion

Leader: We thank you, God, for Jesus and for his example of loving service. We thank you that even on the night in which he was betrayed, he took a loaf of bread *(hold up the bread)*, and when he had given thanks, he broke it *(break the bread)* and said, "This is my body, which is given for you. Do this to remember me." *(The bread is passed around. When finished, hold up a wine cup.)* In the same way, Jesus took the cup after supper and said, "This cup is the new covenant between God and you that has been set in motion by my blood. Do this in remembrance of me, whenever you drink it." *(The wine or juice is passed around.)*

Liturgy for the Walk of the Cross

"After mocking him, they stripped him of the robe and put his own clothes on him. Then they led him away to crucify him. As they went out, they came upon a man from Cyrene named Simon; they compelled this man to carry his cross" (Matthew 27:31–32, NRSV). Not much is known about Simon of Cyrene. Mark, in his gospel, says that he was the father of Alexander and Rufus. That may have been helpful for Mark's church, but since we don't know Alexander and Rufus, it doesn't help us much.

We do know that Cyrene was in northern Africa, in what is now Libya. So we can assume that he was black and since he was coming to Jerusalem that he was Jewish. Like many in those days he may have been a person with no land. During times of occupation the land is taken. Simon (like others forced off the land) is now simply one of many who find themselves at the side of the road. That is where the landless end up, beside the road where beggars and others sit. Today, if we choose to take up the cross, we need to identify with the ones, like Simon of Cyrene, who are at the side of the road and on the margins of our society. Who are marginalized today? Who bears the cross in our society or community today?

Prayer for Good Friday: Compassionate God, we pray for all those who suffer in our world – those we have named and all those whom we cannot name.

Written by Rev. David Martyn. Used by permission.

The Stones Shout Out

Make These Stones into Bread

Reader #1: The Bible is full of images of rocks. If you have ever been to Palestine, it's not difficult to understand why. The country where Jesus grew up is hilly and rocky. So the Hebrew people frequently employed images of rocks and stones in their poems and songs or as metaphors in their writings. For them, rocks symbolized danger and strength. Rocks were valuable because of the copper and other ores found in them. Rocks were symbolically – and in a real sense – dangerous. Rocks were used to stone people. Rocky caves in the desert hid thieves who attacked merchant caravans and travelers on their way to the cities. When Jesus was tempted in the desert, Satan said to him, "Throw yourself from this cliff and God will give orders to the angels; they will hold you up with their hands so that not even your feet will be hurt on the stones."

Reader #2: Read Luke 4:1–13

(Reader #1 and Reader #2 place their rocks in the center to begin the creation of a rock altar/cairn.)

The Stones Shout Out

Reader #1: Rocks and stones are ancient symbols for God – for God's permanence and stability. Altars were often built with uncut stone and used to make sacrifices to God. The Israelites built altars to draw near to God's presence. In some cultures, like Korean and Latin American, stone altars are used to mark the places where people have died. In Western culture, stone grave markers are placed at burial sites. It is an old Mexican custom to pile up stones in places where people want to remember something has happened. It is likely that the road Jesus took to Jerusalem was bordered by stones, rocks, and boulders that had been cleared from the route.

Reader #2: Read Luke 19:28b–40.

(Reader #1 and Reader #2 place their rocks in the center, adding them to the pile.)

The Destruction of the Temple

Reader #1: In ancient times, it was believed that God resided in the temple. Temples, like most buildings of the time, were constructed from stone. Temples symbolized God's presence and favor toward the people. Many times throughout their history, the Hebrew people had been conquered by other nations and their temples were destroyed. When this happened, the people believed God was no longer with them. Jesus used the image of the temple as a metaphor for his own life and death.

Reader #2: Read John 2:13–21.

(Reader #1 and Reader #2 place their rocks in the center, adding them to the pile.)

The Mount of Olives

Reader #1: The Mount of Olives lies to the east of Jerusalem. Gethsemane, on its western slopes, lies just outside the city walls. Some of this area was used as burial ground for the more affluent. The dead were interred in caves or rock-cut tombs on the slopes. During his last days in Jerusalem, Jesus spent the days teaching in the Temple and the nights on the Mount of Olives.

Reader #2: Read Luke 22:39–46.

(Say the Lord's Prayer together. Then Reader #1 and Reader #2 place their rocks in the center, adding them to the pile.)

Peter's Denial

Reader #1: Read Luke 22:47–62.

Reader #2: Peter, faithful follower of Jesus. Peter, the one whom Jesus called "The Rock," the one on whom he would build his church. But, three times, Peter denied knowing Jesus. Then Peter remembered that at the Last Supper Jesus had said to him that he would deny Jesus three times before the rooster announced that morning had come. "Even if everyone else leaves you, I will not," Peter exclaimed. We can imagine the sinking feeling he must have experienced, knowing what he had done.

(Reader #1 and Reader #2 place their rocks in the center, adding them to the pile.)

Jesus Is Tried by Pilate and Herod

Reader #1: Rulers of the time, like Pilate and Herod, had no respect and little genuine interest in the people they governed. They were interested in increasing their own power and name. Their dealings with people were often ruthless and violent. Their greatest achievements were probably in buildings of stone: restored parts of cities, strengthened forts, the rebuilt Temple, a new aqueduct.

Reader #2: Read Luke 23:1–25.

(Reader #1 and Reader #2 place their rocks in the center, adding them to the pile.)

Jesus Is Crucified

Reader #1: Some scholars believe Jesus' crucifixion took place outside the Damascus gate and north wall of Jerusalem. Nearby is a rocky hill and grotto. Part of it is a skull-like rock that rises up from the ground. It is within sight of what may have been a main roadway at that time.

Reader #2: Read Mark 15:21–24a

(Reader #1 and Reader #2 place their rocks in the center, adding them to the pile.)

The Soldiers Cast Lots

Reader #1: In ancient times, "lots" were cast, like rolling dice. We believe these were usually small stones that were cast or drawn to determine God's will. The soldiers cast lots to see who would have Jesus' clothes, a common practice when people were executed in those days.

Reader #2: Read Mark 15:24b–32.
(Reader #1 and Reader #2 place their rocks in the center, adding them to the pile.)

Jesus Dies

Reader #1: Read Mark 15:33–41.
Reader #2: Many people watched Jesus die. They could do nothing to stop such executions. Any actions would have been futile, ending in their own punishment and, possibly, death. Jesus' followers and closest friends stood watching, perhaps in disbelief, in anger, in sorrow. It was like the end of the world for them.

(Reader #1 and Reader #2 place their rocks in the center, adding them to the pile.)

Jesus Is Buried

Reader #1: Luke 23:50–56.
Reader #2: The actions of Joseph of Arimathea ensured that Jesus' body was properly looked after. Joseph, a reputable man, took the body the same day and placed it in a tomb. Some women followers of Jesus accompanied Joseph. They planned the traditional anointing of the body after they had observed the Jewish Sabbath. While it was too late to help Jesus, Joseph and the women acted courageously, openly showing the authorities that they were associated with Jesus and that they remembered him respectfully.

Think of a time when something wrong or unfair has happened to you or to someone else. What could have been said or done afterward to show where you stood? What risks were there? *(Reflect on this question silently. Then Reader#1 and Reader #2 add their rocks to the pile.)*

Philip's Easter Egg

To dramatize this story you may wish to use empty plastic "eggs" and place the various items inside. Invite the youth to open them as you tell the story. Be sure to save the empty one for the end!)

There was a young boy named Philip, who was born with Down's syndrome, which means his mind didn't grow at the same rate as his body. He was happy, but he knew that he wasn't the same as other children. Philip went to church school every Sunday, and was in a class with nine other 8-year-old boys and girls. Sometimes people aren't very friendly to someone different from themselves. That's how it was with Philip. The teacher carefully included Philip in all the activities, and the children tried very hard, but Philip was not really a part of that group. Philip, of course, did not choose or want to be different; he just was.

At Easter, the teacher had a great idea for a lesson. The teacher had collected 12 of the plastic containers that pantyhose come in – the ones that look like big eggs – to use that Sunday. Each child was given one. It was a beautiful spring day, and the task was to go outside on the church grounds and find a symbol for new life, put it into the plastic egg, and bring it back to the classroom. They would then open and share their new life symbols one by one. They did this and it was glorious. And it was confusing. And it was wild. They ran all around, gathered their symbols, and returned to the classroom.

They put the big eggs on a table and the teacher opened them. In the first one, there was a flower, and the children ooed and aahed. He opened another, and there was a little bud. He opened another and there was a rock. Some children laughed, and some said, "That's crazy. How's a rock supposed to be like new life?" But the girl whose egg it was, spoke up. She said, "I knew all of you would get flowers, and buds, and leaves, and butterflies, and things like that. So I got a rock because I wanted to be different, and for me that's new life." The teacher went on opening the eggs.

He opened the last one, and there was nothing in it. Some children said, "That's silly. Somebody didn't do it right." The teacher felt a tug on his shirt and looked down. Philip was standing beside him. "It's mine," Philip said. "It's mine." And the children said, "You don't ever do things right, Philip. There's nothing there!" "I did so do it," Philip said. "I did do it. It's empty. The tomb is empty." There was silence. Then Jason said, "What a terrific idea." The rest of the children joined in, "Philip had the best surprise." From that time on, Philip became a real part of that group. The whole class discovered new life because they had discovered that every person has something special to give. It didn't matter anymore that Philip was different. They all knew he belonged there.

Philip died the next summer. His family had known since the time that he was born that he wouldn't live out a full life span. Many other things had been wrong with his tiny little body. He was buried from his church. And on that day at the funeral nine 8-year-old children paraded right up to the altar, not with flowers, but with an empty plastic egg. They placed it on the altar in celebration of Philip's new life.

Idea Page # What It Means to Be a Christian

Group Check-in

Ahead of time, ask group members to bring a symbol from home of some group they belong to (e.g. a badge, a team jersey, a pin, a family tartan or crest). Invite group members in turn to show the object they have brought and to explain its significance. What purpose do these symbols have (e.g to identify members of a group, to show pride or achievement)?

Symbols for Christians

The **fish** was used as a symbol by Christian followers in the early church. The acrostic derived from the Greek letters for the word "fish" (*ichthys*) were understood to stand for Jesus Christ, God's Son, the Savior [**I**esous (Jesus) **CH**ristos (Christ) **TH**eou (of God) **U**iou (the Son) **S**oter (the Savior)]. The symbol was simple to draw and was often used among Christians as a type of password during times of persecution by the Roman government. If two strangers met and were unsure whether the other was a Christian, one would draw an arc in the earth like this) . If the other were a Christian, they would complete the symbol with a reverse arc like this () , forming the outline of a fish ><>.

The **cross** did not become a common and recognized symbol of the followers of Christ until the fourth century, when Christianity became the official religion of Rome. Until the reign of Emperor Constantine (306–337), crucifixion was the common penalty for a variety of crimes. Constantine put an end to the practice. The result of this was that crucifixion and the cross itself took on an increasingly symbolic character and significance. The cross, which was an instrument of torture and death, became a symbol of salvation and hope: a sign of Christian faith.

Agree/Disagree

Label one end of the room "Agree" and the opposite end "Disagree." Read statements like the examples below and invite the youth to move to one end of the room or the other to indicate if they agree or disagree with the statement: "A Christian is someone who..."

- Attends church
- Reads the Bible regularly
- Tries to live according to the values that Jesus modeled
- Believes Jesus is the only way to God
- Believes in the Virgin Birth
- Doesn't lie, steal, or cheat others

Montage Cross

You will need: cardboard or box board, a variety of art and craft supplies or "found" materials such as buttons, bottle caps, small toys, etc.

Look at crosses from different cultures such as Coptic, Latin American, Celtic, and the examples from **The Christian Symbol of the Cross** on page 108. Invite group members to design their own cross. Begin by using the cardboard or sturdy box board to create the base – the cross shape. Use your imagination to decorate this in a way that is meaningful. Here are just a few suggestions:

- Glue pieces of an old jigsaw puzzle in an interesting pattern. Overlap pieces for a three-dimensional look. If you wish to paint these after the glue has dried, glue the puzzle pieces picture-side down.

- Appliquéing is done by cutting out shapes of material and arranging them on the surface of other material to form a design.

- Collage is the artistic technique of applying manufactured, printed, or "found" materials, such as bits of newspaper, fabric, wallpaper, comic books, movie magazines, and advertising.

Who Wants to Be a Disciple?

The name "disciple" was given to Jesus' earliest followers. The word comes from the Latin *discipulus*, "learner" (from *discere*, to learn). Being a learner is an important part of being Christian. No matter what age we are, we are all learning and growing in faith. Play this fun variation of the popular TV game show *Who Wants to Be a Millionaire?* See pages 115–116 for what you need, how to play, and some sample questions.

Cyberspace Scavenger Hunt

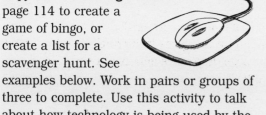

Plan a trip to an Internet café. Copy the blank **Bingo Card** from page 114 to create a game of bingo, or create a list for a scavenger hunt. See examples below. Work in pairs or groups of three to complete. Use this activity to talk about how technology is being used by the church to communicate with members, reach others, and conduct other practical activities. If your church doesn't already have a website, the group might take this on as a project. A good place to begin is to utilize the free tools at ForMinistry.com, a website project of the American Bible Society that provides every Christian church in North America with a free entry in their searchable directory of churches.

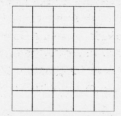

Sample Descriptions

• Found the official website of our denomination

• Found our church website

• Checked out today's cartoon at Reverend Fun at www.gospelcom.net/rev-fun

• Found someone who knows what http stands for

• Found a website for Christian youth

• Read a movie review at www.hollywoodjesus.com

• Checked to see if our church is registered in the free church locator listings at www.forministry.com

• Clicked on a dead link

• Someone ordered a beverage with enough caffeine in it to keep them awake for several days

Outreach Clue Hunt

Most churches have outreach ministries that many people in the congregation are not aware of, such as a place to collect food or clothing, a thrift shop, a food shelf with emergency supplies, a discretionary fund (money usually administered by church staff to people in need), tape ministries to shut-ins, a place where old pairs of eyeglasses are collected to support Focus on Sight, or where used stamps or Campbell's soup "Labels for Education" are collected. Your church may also make space available to groups such as Alcoholics Anonymous, Compassionate Friends, or for a group for pregnant teens, etc. Create a set of clues that leads from one place (where items are actually gathered, or to a symbolic location) to another. Begin by reading out the first clue (e.g. "This is where you'd find food to give a hungry person who came to our church for help.") When they locate the place (e.g. food pantry), they should find the next clue taped somewhere nearby. This clue will instruct them to find the next location and the next clue, and so on.

Afterwards discuss:

• Read Matthew 25:31–40. How does our church try to live out this passage?

• Who besides those mentioned here might be considered "the least of these" in our society? How might we reach out to them?

• When have you been hungry, thirsty, a stranger, in need of clothes, sick or imprisoned, and someone reached out to you?

• How do you think these actions help not only others, but those who do them?

Closing Worship

Lay long strips of colored fabric on the floor in a cross-shape. Place tea lights or small votive candles in glass holders at points on the cross. Sing or listen to a recording of a song.

Prayer:

Jesus, you were filled with passion and conviction
that people did not understand,
that people feared,
that people ignored.
Sometimes the things that matter to me
don't seem to matter to anyone else,
but I know they matter to you and to God.
Grant me courage to live out the convictions
that burn inside of me. Amen.

The Christian Symbol of the Cross

Graded Cross

The 3 steps represent faith, hope, and charity (Cor. 13:13).

Maltese Cross

This is the emblem of John the Baptist. Its 8 points stand for the 8 Beatitudes (Matthew 5:3–12).

Anchor Cross

The top part of an anchor is a cross, showing Christ, our anchor and hope (Hebrews 6:19).

Egyptian Cross

This symbol means "life" in Egyptian hieroglyphics. It was adopted by the Coptic Christians (in Egypt) because Christ is "The Tree of Life."

The Celtic cross

symbolizes the spiritual world (vertical axis) and the physical world (horizontal axis). When they meet in the center a balance is achieved creating a sense of wholeness. Hence the circle, which is a symbol for oneness, and a symbol for God.

The Jerusalem Cross

adds four small crosses to the corners of one large Greek cross. This combination of five crosses represents the five wounds of Christ. Eleventh- and Twelfth-century pilgrims to Jerusalem adopted this symbol as a favorite emblem.

Greek Cross

The 4 arms are of equal length. This is the symbol used by the Red Cross to stand for peace and neutrality.

Budded Cross

The 3 buds at each arm represent growth and new life; 3 also stands for the Trinity – God who is father, Son, and Holy Spirit.

Idea Page

Jubilee: Renewal of the Earth

Group Check-in

Choose an animal that represents how you are feeling right now. Take turns explaining your choice to the other group members. (e.g. "Right now I am feeling like a mouse, sort of timid and quiet.")

Did you know?

The first Earth Day was held to promote environmental awareness and to protest pollution, in 1970, the same year the Environmental Protection Agency was formed.

Slide Prayers

Create a short slide show that could be incorporated into the prayers of intercession in worship. You will need at least two sessions to complete this project. Plan a time to take photographs. Divide into small groups and provide each with a camera and a roll of slide film. (This film costs slightly more than regular film but is specifically intended to create slides. Ask for it at your local photography store.) Ask groups to take pictures of trees, flowers, beaches, or other things that symbolize the concerns of the group about the environment (e.g. the local dump, cars/traffic, road signs that warn of danger to animals). Plan to meet again after the slides have been developed, to view them and to write prayers to accompany them. Show the slides during worship, taking turns reading the prayers while the images are shown.

Banners

Create a banner for Earth Day or Rogation Sunday using this simple technique or see page 122 for instructions for batiking banners.

You will need: solid-colored fabric (blue and green work best), assorted natural objects (leaves, ferns, flowers), rubber gloves, spray bottle, bleach, bucket, water

Instructions: Lay the fabric outdoors on a hard, flat surface, such as cement, away from anything that might be damaged by bleach. Arrange the leaves, flowers, and other objects in a simple design on the fabric. Only the silhouettes of the items will show, so objects with distinctive shapes work best. If there's a breeze, place stones on the objects to hold them in place. Wearing rubber gloves, spray the fabric lightly with bleach around all the edges of the design. Let the fabric set until you see the color start to change, about one minute or so. Carefully remove and dispose of the flowers and leaves. Submerge the banner in a bucket of water and thoroughly rinse it. This stops the bleach from eating through the fabric. Put it through the washer and dryer, and your masterpiece is ready!

Jubilee: Give It a Rest!

We live in a time of intense technological, scientific, and economic change. The Earth is suffering the effects of the overuse and over-fertilization of farm land, poisoning of rivers and lakes with mining and industrial waste, deforestation, acid rain and air pollution caused by fossil fuels, and the extinction of whole species of animals through destruction of their habitats. If everyone in the world consumed resources at the same rate that North Americans do, we would need two additional planets the size of the Earth in order for everyone to survive. In Leviticus, the vision of Jubilee calls for people to give the land a "rest" – to leave fields crop-free, and to leave vineyards unpruned. Instead, the people were to eat only what the earth provided in the Jubilee Year.

Global Issues

Make copies of the following list for each participant. Invite them to look at a list of issues. Then give them the following instructions: "Study the list of problems facing the world. Rank them according to their importance to you and then compare and discuss the different priorities."

Forests
Energy
Waste
Debt
Poverty
Security (War)
Population
Trade
Aid
Water
Endangered species
Disease
Employment
Crime
Drugs
Pollution

Afterwards, discuss as a group:

- What do you feel is the highest priority? The lowest? Why?

- How can we address this issue by our actions?

- Do you think people in other countries would rank these differently? How? Why?

The Earth Pledge

The Earth Pledge was drafted during the Earth Summit held in Rio de Janeiro, Brazil, in 1992. If your group is planning to participate in worship, write the Earth Pledge – "To help make the Earth a secure and hospitable home for present and future generations" – on a long strip of banner paper and invite people to sign it as a gesture of their commitment to caring for the Earth. This might be part of the Offering.

Service Project

Plan a project that the whole group can participate in, such as cleaning a beach in your area, planting a tree, holding a recycling drive/collection, or participating in an Adopt-a-Road project.

Garbage Scavenger Hunt

This is a good activity for get-togethers at a beach or picnic/park area. Give the youth a garbage bag and a list of items that must be found on the ground. Taking from garbage cans is not allowed! Points are awarded for each item and there is no limit for the amount of items retrieved. Also, award bonus points for the most different items on the list that are collected. For example, if anyone brings in at least one of every item on the list, they might get a bonus of 100 points. Sample items: 1. Candy wrapper 2. Aluminum beverage can 3. Plastic fork 4. Paper cup 5. Gum wrapper 6. Pop or beer bottle, etc.

Additional resources

Earth Prayers: 365 Prayers, Poems, and Invocations for Honoring the Earth edited by Elizabeth Roberts and Elias Amidon (San Francisco, HarperSanFrancisco, 1991).
http://www.web.net/~tendays/youth.html Ten Days for Global Justice

---

Closing Worship

Create a sand or earth table. Place a candle in the center. Bring a variety of natural items that might be incorporated, such as leaves, pinecones, twigs, rocks, shells, driftwood.

Prayer:

Generous God,
thank you for the earth and all the gifts
that we receive from the earth.
Help us to be good caretakers of
the earth and of each other.
In Jesus' name we pray. Amen.

Retreats and Wind-ups

Group Games and Mixers

Stand Up If You…

This is a good game for groups of any size.

Instructions: Everyone sits in a large circle. Call out descriptions, beginning with the phrase "Stand up if you…(e.g. ate breakfast this morning)." If the statement describes them, the youth should stand. Descriptions should be fun, but can also be useful. For example, at a youth event you might ask all the youth from the host congregation to stand. Have everyone look around and notice who they are; these are people who know where bathrooms are, how to find things, etc. Some other examples:

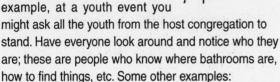

Stand up if you…

… have a pet.

… have been in youth group for at least a year.

… have ever written a letter to Santa Claus.

… know how to pronounce your name backwards.

People to People

This is a good mixer game, especially for people who don't already know each other, such as at a large youth retreat or event.

Instructions: A large group of people mingles in a designated area. The facilitator has people chant "People to People" while snapping their fingers (you choose the rhythm). The facilitator then calls out a specific number of people and asks them to build something with others, or to do an action. For example, the facilitator might say, "Three people make a washing machine." All participants gather into groups and complete the request. After a few things have been called out, repeat one of the previous requests so that people have to remember and find the same group they originally did that action with.

Examples:
- build a shower (3 people)
- build a car (5 people)
- build an airplane (10 people)
- build a working McDonald's (20 people)
- build a roller coaster using the whole group.

Outdoor Retreats

Worship under the Stars

As the sky becomes dark, gather in a spot where most of the sky will be visible with no interference from bright lights. Identify any bright stars (planets) or constellations (Orion, Big Dipper) or the Milky Way. Imagine you are shepherds living in the time of Jesus. You study these stars every night. Can you make up a story about one of the groups of stars you see? Share stories or have one person start a story and go around the circle, each person adding a sentence to the tale. Read Psalm 8 as a shepherd in Bible times might have recited it.

Hiker's Bingo

Use the blank **Bingo Card** from page 114. Create a bingo sheet. Adapt it to your camp's natural setting. Players place an "X" in the appropriate square when they find an item on the card. The object is to fill in all squares. Agree on a time limit and on the distance that players may travel, or play the game as a group on a hike. Examples of objects to find: animal track, stream or river, squirrel, acorn, litter, seashell, pine tree, sparrow, red flower, butterfly, ant.

Plaster Sand Casting

By using scooped out damp sand as a mold, you can make these plaster keepsakes in a backyard sandbox or at the beach.

You will need: powdered plaster of Paris and coffee cans to mix it in, damp sand, shells, rocks, driftwood, etc.

Instructions: Using your hands, scoop out wet sand to make a mold that is about 6 inches wide, 12 inches long, and 2 inches deep, in the shape of a fish, cross, footprint, or whatever other symbol you choose. While the sand is still damp, if desired, press shells, rocks, and driftwood into the bottom of the mold. Fill the coffee can 2/3 full of water and add dry plaster until it mounds up above the water. Stir with your hand and wait five minutes before pouring. Carefully pour plaster into the mold. Let it harden for an hour. Lift the plaster shape out of the mold and brush off the loose sand.

Batik Banners

Make beautiful individual banners or a banner for your sanctuary. This is a  project that requires lots of space and it can be a bit messy. Perfect for outdoor or indoor retreats where you have lots of time and space. See page 122 for instructions.

Letter to Myself

Before the end of the retreat, invite the youth to write a letter to themselves about what they enjoyed about the retreat, what they learned, and what they are taking away from the experience. Provide envelopes. Have youth print their address on the front and seal the envelope. Mail these two or three weeks after the retreat ends.

Confirmation Retreats

Most denominations have a process leading up to Confirmation or Renewal of Baptism Vows. It may require participation in a membership class and include an introduction to the basic doctrines or beliefs of a particular denomination (view of the Bible, denominational history, etc.). Whatever your particular tradition, a final retreat can be a good way to conclude this process. Plan a retreat that includes only youth, or youth and their adult mentors. Include activities that help participants explore their own beliefs about God, Jesus, the Bible, the church. Also include time for confirmands to help plan the service, such as designing a meaningful ritual, exploring the questions they will be asked to answer, discussing the meaning of symbols and symbolic actions used in Confirmation.

Mentors

Pairing confirmands with mentors can strengthen the confirmand's understanding of the faith while connecting him or her with the community of believers in a personal way. You may wish to involve mentors prior to the retreat by having confirmand and mentor write letters back and forth, or communicate by e-mail. Suggested questions: What is your favorite Bible story? What is a question you struggle with about God, Jesus, the Bible? Why do you come to church? Describe an experience you've had that has shaped your faith/beliefs... My spiritual high point (when I felt closest to God)... My spiritual low point (when I felt most distant from God)... Special people who have played a role in my faith journey...

Wind-up Retreats and Group Closure
The Year in Review

This is a fun, creative way to evaluate what you've done as a group over the past year. Have group members imagine the year as a movie they've just seen and are reviewing. You may wish to write the questions down on paper and give each group member a copy. This could be done individually or by small groups and presented as a skit. Give them time to think about their answers. Then share the "reviews."

- Give the year a title (e.g. The Big Thrill, Fun and Funner, Mission Incredible)
- Pick a clip (i.e. name a highlight)
- Comment on the plot and theme (i.e. activities the group did)
- Comment on the actors (participants) and producer-director (leaders)

Affirmation Collages

This affirming exercise is for groups that have gotten to know each other well over the year.

You will need: newsprint, magazines, scissors, glue, markers

Instructions: Have everyone look through magazines for words or pictures that describe qualities and strengths they admire in other members of the group. Encourage everyone to find at least one word or picture for each person in the group. Write the name of each group member on a piece of newsprint. Pass these sheets around the circle one by one so group members can glue on the clippings and explain their contribution. Then present the collage to the person it describes.

Additional resources

The Story of the Bible: How the World's Bestselling Book Came to Be by Cheryl Perry (Kelowna, BC: Wood Lake Books, 1999) Makes a great program for a retreat or Confirmation class. Material for youth and adults includes lots of fun activities, including a Bible Jeopardy game, research activities, quizzes, and projects.
Making Disciples by William Willimon (Inver Grove Heights, MN: Logos Productions) Based on the mentorship model, *Making Disciples* can be used as a stand-alone program, or in conjunction with your current curriculum as a special experiential unit. Topics covered include: God, Jesus, Holy Spirit, Worship, The Bible, Saints and Gifts, Ministry, Baptism, Spiritual Life, Death and Resurrection, Life in the Church, and The Faith Journey Continues.

Appendix

Bingo Card

Who Wants to Be a Disciple?

This is a spin-off of the popular TV game show *Who Wants to Be a Millionaire?* Contestants are quizzed on their knowledge of the Bible and church year as they try to win the million-dollar prize. Questions have multiple-choice answers; players must choose the correct response to advance to the next dollar sum. The first question is worth $100 and values increase to $200, $500, $1,000, $2,000, $5,000, $10,000, $20,000, $50,000, $100,000, $500,000, and finally to $1,000,000. Of course, being that they are disciples, they can't keep the money for themselves! So begin each new round by asking contestants what they would do if they won the grand prize. How would they use the money to further God's reign of Shalom?

You will need: play money, a 60-second timer

Instructions: Create multiple-choice questions appropriate to the age and skill level of your group. As in the examples below, questions should become progressively more difficult as their dollar value increases. Players have three lifelines to use as necessary to come up with the correct response: 50/50 (remove two wrong answers so the person has a 50/50 chance), Survey the Audience (the audience votes for what it thinks is the correct response), and Ask a Friend with a Bible (any other player can be asked to look something up in the Bible).

$100

The name of Jesus' father
a. Ben Hur
b. Joseph
c. John
d. Regis

The place of Jesus' birth
a. Tel Aviv
b. Mount Sinai
c. Bethlehem
d. Bethany

The celebration of Jesus' birth is called
a. Hanukkah
b. Christmas
c. Advent
d. Reign of Christ

$200

The name of the church season that consists of the 40 days leading up to Easter
a. Lent
b. Advent
c. Pentecost
d. Holy Week

The name of the first book of the Bible
a. Book of Job
b. Book of Bob
c. The Book of Genesis
d. Guinness Book of World Records

What is the special color of the season of Lent?
a. purple
b. orange
c. green
d. black

$500

The name of the sacred scriptures of the Christian faith
a. the Bible
b. the Torah
c. the Koran
d. the Talmud

Jesus' father's occupation
a. plumber
b. tax collector
c. carpenter
d. bus driver

The Magi found Jesus, Mary, and Joseph by following
a. an angel
b. a star
c. a map
d. a trail of breadcrumbs

The name of the Disney movie that tells the story of Moses
a. Prince of Tides
b. Prince of Thieves
c. The Little Prince
d. Prince of Egypt

$1,000

The customary response to the greeting "God be with you"
a. Bless you
b. Amen
c. Thank you
d. And also with you

John the Baptist was what kind of relative to Jesus?
a. uncle
b. cousin
c. step-brother
d. second cousin once removed on his mother's side

Which of these gifts was NOT presented to Jesus by the Magi?
a. gold
b. myrrh oil
c. incense
d. diamonds

$2,000

The name of the king who tried to have Jesus killed when he was just a baby
a. Herod
b. Moses
c. Ramses II
d. Macbeth

The name of the mountain where Moses received the 10 Commandments
a. Mount Manna
b. Mount Quail
c. Mount of Olives
d. Mount Sinai

What was the symbol of God's promise never to destroy the earth again?
a. a rainbow
b. the number 40
c. pillar of fire
d. burning bush

$5,000

Moses' sister was a prophet. What was her name?
a. Mariah
b. Miriam
c. Martha
d. Minnie

The book of the Bible that you would find the story of Moses in

a. Book of Daniel   c. Book of Kings
b. Ezekiel   d. Exodus

What did Noah take on the Ark with him besides his family?

a. flotation devices   c. two of each kind of animal
b. a Bible   d. some dirt

$10,000

Which of the following people was NOT one of Jesus' disciples?

a. Thomas   c. John
b. Peter   d. Namaan

Which of these women is a book of the Bible named after?

a. Jezebel   c. Sarah
b. Sheila   d. Ruth

He heard God calling him in the middle of the night and he thought it was his master, the priest Eli.

a. Jesus   c. Frederick
b. Saul   d. Samuel

$20,000

What was the name of the disciple who betrayed Jesus to the Roman authorities with a kiss?

a. Gerald   c. James
b. Zacchaeus   d. Judas

Which of the following is NOT a miracle performed by Jesus?

a. walking on water
b. turning water into blood
c. turning water into wine
d. feeding 5,000 people with two loaves and five fish

What is the name of the Jewish holiday that Jesus was celebrating with his disciples on the night before he died?

a. Passover   c. St. Patrick's Day
b. Shavot   d. Shrove Tuesday

$50,000

Which of the following is the name of an Old Testament prophet?

a. Isaiah   c. Nostradamus
b. Nicodemus   d. John the Baptist

What did people wave as they saw Jesus entering Jerusalem, riding on a donkey?

a. the flag of Israel   c. fig leaves
b. palm branches   d. purple ribbons

Which of the following foods is associated with the Passover meal, celebrating the escape of the Hebrew people from Egypt?

a. frog's legs   c. figs
b. unleavened bread   d. roasted pork

$100,000

In Jesus' time, the scriptures were written on these, not in books as the Bible is today

a. towels   c. leaves
b. scrolls   d. clay tablets

The number of books in the Bible

a. ten   c. thirty-three
b. twelve   d. sixty-six

Who wrote a great number of letters that we read in the Bible?

a. the apostle Paul   c. Jesus
b. Adam   d. Anne Landers

$500,000

Of the following four statements about Jesus, which of them is NOT true?

a. Jesus became a refugee when he was 2 years old. He and his family fled to Egypt.
b. The Bible says Jesus had brothers and sisters.
c. Jesus healed a man on the Sabbath, the Jewish holy day, which was against the law.
d. The apostle Paul was one of Jesus' twelve disciples.

A book of the Bible where we would find the story of Jesus' birth.

a. Gospel of Luke   c. Gospel of Mark
b. Book of Acts   d. Book of Revelation

The name of the city God told Jonah to go to, but he refused

a. Ninevah   c. Kelowna
b. Troas   d. Syria

$1,000,000

Legend says that when Jesus was crucified, this was used to catch the blood that poured from a wound in his side

a. a ram's horn   c. the Holy Sponge
b. the Holy Grail   d. the Shroud of Turin

In 1945 some scrolls, the oldest known manuscripts of the Bible, were found in a cave near which sea?

a. Sea of Galilee   c. Red Sea
b. Sea of Tranquility   d. Dead Sea

What is the name of the Jewish coin used in the Temple?

a. dime   c. denarius
b. shekel   d. peso

Answers: 100—b, c, b; 200—a, c, a; 500—a, c, b, d; 1000—d, d; 2000—a, d, a; 5000—b, d, c: 10000—d, d; 20000—d, b, a; 50000—a, b, b; 100000—b, d, a: 500000—d, a, a; 1000000—b, d, b

Alternative Monopoly

Copy both sets of cards and cut them apart. These will replace the Community Chest and Chance Cards. Play one game as a lesser-developed country and another game as a more-developed country.

CARDS FOR LESSER-DEVELOPED COUNTRIES

SOLD CASH CROPS
Your family sold all of your pineapples, oranges, and mangoes to another country.
Collect $350

CHILD LABOR
Your youngest daughter drops out of school to work. Her salary increases the entire family's income.
Collect $150

LAND PRESSURES
There are increased demands on land with a growing population. You may have only houses and no hotels on all of your properties.

GARBAGE DUMPING FEES
Other countries are paying to dump their waste in your village.
Collect $75

MUDSLIDES
An entire village was lost in a mudslide caused by heavy rain. Remove all of your houses and hotels from 2 properties of your choice.

HURRICANE SEASON
A storm has damaged some of your property. You must reduce your hotel rental fee by 50%.

DOCTOR'S FEE
You have developed an illness after spraying pesticides on bananas.
Pay $150

INSURANCE INCREASE
After the last damaging flood, insurance companies have increased their premiums (fees).
Pay $200

ANIMAL INCOME
You sold your family's cow to generate more cash for your family.
Collect $100

INFLATION
The dollar has dropped in value. You cannot afford to keep all of your properties. Remove half of your houses.

EDUCATION FEES
Your 4 children need new uniforms, new books, and tuition fees for another term.
Pay $500

LOST DAYS
You became ill for several weeks after drinking unclean water from the river. You lose your full salary. Do not collect money the next time that you pass "go."

CARDS FOR MORE-DEVELOPED COUNTRIES

INDUSTRY CHANGES
You have been laid off and rehired in another job that pays a lower salary. **Collect $100 (not $200) whenever you pass "go."**

TAX HIKE
Taxes have been increased because of the rising cost of health care. **Pay $250**

BANK FEES
The next time you pass "Go," pay your fees to the bank. The bank does not pay you.

STOCK MARKET COLLAPSE
The value of stocks in your company suddenly drop. Do not collect money the next time you pass "go."

LAND PRESSURES
There are increased demands on land with a growing population. You may have only houses and no hotels on all of your properties.

WARMER WEATHER
Higher temperatures due to global warming have led to an increase in food production in your country and a better economy. **Collect $300**

HOUSING COSTS
You need to make upgrades on your houses. **Pay $100 for every house and $150 for every hotel you own.**

TAX REBATE
Your business receives a tax rebate because of environmentally friendly practices. **Collect $75**

FOSSIL FUELS
Advance token to the next railroad. **Pay the owner ten times the rental to which she or he is otherwise entitled.** (If the railroad is unowned, you may buy it from the bank at 3 times the market value.)

CLEAN WATER ACT
The government has passed a law that states that you must install additional water purification systems in all of your buildings. **Pay $250 for every hotel.**

ENVIRONMENTAL REFUGEES
Environmental refugees relocate into your neighborhood. Downgrade all hotel rental fees by 50% for the rest of the game.

TOXIC WASTE FINE
The processor of the toxic waste pays. **Pay $125 for every house you own.**

Christmas Quiz

What does the Bible *really* say?

*(Circle your answer—
more than one may be right.)*

1. **Mary and Joseph went to Bethlehem because:**
   a. that was the city where King David was born.
   b. Joseph had to pay his taxes.
   c. Mary was about to have her baby and wanted to be near her relatives.
   d. Joseph had to register for the census in the home-town of his ancestors.
   e. they wanted to celebrate a religious holiday there.

2. **How did Mary and Joseph travel to Bethlehem?**
   a. on a camel
   b. on a donkey
   c. walked
   d. Joseph walked, Mary rode a donkey.
   e. no one knows.

3. **When Mary and Joseph arrived in Bethlehem...**
   a. they went from inn to inn looking for a place to stay.
   b. they discovered there was no room for them to stay in the inn.
   c. a kind innkeeper invited them to stay in his stable.
   d. they didn't have any money to stay at the inn so they asked to sleep in the stable.

4. **Jesus was born in:**
   a. a stable
   b. a hospital
   c. a cave
   d. a house
   e. unknown

5. **A "manger" is a...**
   a. loft of a barn
   b. wooden hay storage bin
   c. feeding trough
   d. place where the animals are kept

6. **Which animals does the Bible say were present at Jesus' birth?**
   a. cows, donkeys, sheep
   b. a lamb and a donkey
   c. goats, sheep, cows
   d. we aren't told

7. **When Mary gave birth to Jesus she was:**
   a. married to Joseph
   b. engaged to Joseph
   c. living with Joseph
   d. about 14 years old

8. **Who saw the "star in the east"?**
   a. shepherds
   b. Mary and Joseph
   c. three kings
   d. King Herod
   e. none of the above
   f. all of the above

9. **How many angels spoke to the shepherds?**
   a. one
   b. three
   c. a "multitude"

10. **What were the shepherds told would "prove" that the message was true?**
    a. They'd see a star over Bethlehem.
    b. They'd see a baby wrapped in swaddling cloths.
    c. They'd find a baby lying in a manger.
    d. all of the above

11. **The wise men wanted to find Jesus in order to...**
    a. warn his parents about Herod's plans to kill Jesus
    b. worship him
    c. give him gifts

12. **The wise men found Jesus in ...**
    a. a stable
    b. a house
    c. an inn
    d. we don't know

13. **The wise men presented Jesus with gifts of...**
    a. toys and jewels
    b. gold, frankincense, and myrrh
    c. items they got in Africa

14. **How many wise men came to see Jesus?**
    a. two
    b. three
    c. four
    d. we aren't told

15. **How did King Herod find out where Jesus had been born?**
    a. The wise men told him.
    b. He saw the star.
    c. The royal astronomers saw the star and told him about it.
    d. He had a dream about it.
    e. The chief priests and teachers of the Law searched the scriptures and told him.

16. **The story of Jesus' birth is found in:**
    a. all 4 gospels
    b. only in Matthew and Luke
    c. only in Matthew and Mark
    d. only in John's Gospel

Take this home and try it on your family!

Answers to the
"Christmas Quiz –
What does the Bible *really* say?"

1. **A** and **D**.
   Joseph had to register for the census in the city his ancestors came from. Joseph went to Bethlehem, the birthplace of King David, because he was a descendant of David. (Luke 2:1–4)

2. **E**.
   We don't really know how Joseph and Mary got to Bethlehem from Nazareth and the Bible gives us no account of their trip. People through the ages have imagined them traveling on foot or by donkey and have depicted them this way in paintings and sculptures. (Luke 2:4)

3. **B**.
   The Bible records that "there was no room for them to stay in the inn" but it doesn't tell us that Mary and Joseph went from inn to inn and were turned away or that any innkeeper took pity on them because Mary was pregnant. The mention of Mary laying the child in a "manger" likely led people in later times to assume Jesus was born in some sort of stable. In ancient times however, stables as we know them didn't exist. Instead, animals were kept in the enclosed courtyards of inns or in nearby caves. It is possible that Mary and Joseph were forced to sleep in such a place when they found no room in the inn.

4. **E**.
   See answer above.

5. **C**.

6. **D**.
   The mention of the "manger" in which Mary laid the baby suggests that Mary and Joseph had to sleep among the animals, but no mention of them is made in the Bible.

7. **A, B,** and **D**.
   According to Matthew, they were married. But Luke says they were just engaged. Scholars suggest that Mary was about 14 years old.

8. **E**.
   The wise men or Magi saw the star in the east, but they were not kings. (Matthew 2:1)

9. **A**.
   Only one angel spoke to the shepherds. The others appeared "singing praises to God."

10. **C**.
    All babies were wrapped in swaddling cloths but this baby was unusual in that it was lying in a manger.

11. **B**.
    They came to worship him (Matt. 2:2). The gifts were part of their homage or worship. The wise men did not know of Herod's plans to kill the baby. Herod told them to return to Jerusalem after they had found Jesus and tell him where the child was so that Herod, too, could go to worship him. The wise men were warned in a dream not to return to Herod, but to go home another way.

12. **B**.
    The star appeared in the east at about the time of Jesus' birth. It is likely that the wise men did not arrive in Judea until Jesus was almost 2 years old, since it was children 2 years old and under that Herod had put to death. We are told that they found the child and his parents in a *house* in Bethlehem. (Matt. 2:11)

13. **B**.
    Frankincense is a fragrant resin from certain trees in Asia or Africa that gives off a sweet, spicy odor when burned. Myrrh is a fragrant, gummy substance from trees found in Arabia and East Africa. It has a bitter taste and is used in medicines, perfumes, and incense. So "C" might also be correct but the Bible doesn't tell us.

14. **D**.
    The Bible account does not tell us how many wise men (Magi) there were. The traditional representation of 3 likely began because we are told that they brought 3 gifts – gold, frankincense and myrrh. (Matthew 2:1–11)

15. **E**.
    When the wise men came to ask Herod where they might find the baby born to be "the King of the Jews" Herod called together the chief priests and teachers of the Law and asked them. They told him what the prophet Micah had written: that the Messiah would be born in Bethlehem. (Matthew 2:3–6/Micah 5:2)

16. **B**.
    Only 2 of the 4 gospels in our Bible tell the story of Jesus' birth – Matthew and Luke. John speaks symbolically of light coming into the world to describe Jesus' coming (birth).

Name That Carol

Batik Banners

Make individual banners or a banner for your sanctuary. The word *batik* (pronounced bah-teek) means "wax written." It is a way to decorate cloth by covering part of it with a coat of wax and then dyeing the cloth. The waxed area keeps its original color and when the wax is removed the contrast between the dyed and undyed area makes the pattern.

You will need: a large piece of plain white cotton fabric, paraffin wax, beeswax, a tin can, large saucepan, paint brushes, cold-water fabric dyes, an iron, paper towels or clean newsprint. Arrange for a hotplate or access to a kitchen.

Instructions: Prepare cold-water dye according to instructions on the package. Place wax in a can, and the can in a saucepan with about 3 in. (7 cm) water in the bottom. Boil water until wax is bubbling gently, then turn heat to low. (N.B. Never melt wax in a can directly on the burner because this is a fire hazard.) If you wish, use a pencil to draw a simple design on the fabric. (If you are designing a banner for Pentecost, this might be a dove and flames – symbols of the Holy Spirit.) Use the paint brushes to apply wax onto those areas you wish to remain undyed. You can also make dots and lines by dripping wax directly on to the cloth from lighted candles. Because batik wax is applied hot, it is necessary to work fairly quickly. Do not go over the same place twice – this has no effect – but paint on boldly, continually renewing the flow of wax on your brush. When wax is cool, crumple the fabric a little to encourage the wax to "vein" (crack). This creates the batik effect. Immerse the fabric into the dye bath for the period of time suggested by the manufacturer. (Optional: To add a second color of dye, let the fabric dry completely and apply wax to the area where you wish to keep the first color, and repeat dyeing process.) When fabric has dried, remove wax by ironing fabric between layers of paper towels or newsprint. Finish the banner by folding the top edge over a dowel and sewing or stapling so it can be hung.

TIP: Use 100% cotton fabric for best results.

N.B. Do not use hot-water dyes as these will cause the hardened wax to melt in the dye bath.

TIP: Beeswax adheres well to fabric, whereas paraffin wax is brittle, cracking easily. The ideal mixture for batik is about 30% beeswax, 70% paraffin.

N.B. The key is to get the wax hot enough that when it is applied to the fabric the wax completely penetrates the fabric. This is tricky, because the wax dries rapidly on the brush and must therefore be applied quickly. It is important to keep the wax hot while you are working, so if possible keep the pot on an electric burner or portable camp stove. If you have difficulty, before you place the fabric in the dye bath, hold it over a steaming kettle and allow the steam to remelt the wax. This is effective, but causes the design to "spread" somewhat.

Making a Masking Tape Labyrinth

Labyrinths have been used since the Middle Ages to enable people to focus and reflect.

You will need: a large uncarpeted area in which to lay out the labyrinth, masking tape

Instructions: Lay the masking tape on the floor to create a spiral path, moving outward from the center (see diagram). There should be room for people to walk along the path without bumping into anyone coming the other way.

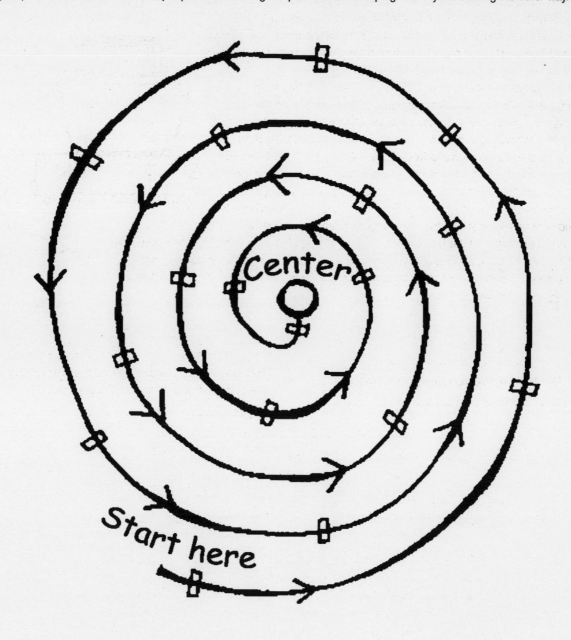

To create a more elaborate 11-circuit labyrinth with masking tape, visit
http://labyrinthproject.com/tape-cpl.html for instructions.

Fundraising Ideas

Why do youth groups fundraise?

Well to raise money, of course, but...the reality is that today's tight church budgets often require that if youth groups want to do something special (such as a retreat) they'll need to fundraise. Fundraising has many other benefits such as:

- Helping the group to grow while working together and developing a sense of ownership for the group. Remember, fundraising should also be fun-raising!

- Providing the opportunity for teens to take on responsibility and gain respect from the congregation.

- Increasing commitment and participation. When youth have had the challenge of raising funds for an activity, their level of commitment and participation is generally higher.

Soup, Sandwich, and Sundae Sunday Fundraiser

Ask each group member to donate one or two loaves of sandwiches. Bring made-ahead sandwiches the day of the fundraiser. Serve homemade soup that your group has prepared. End the meal with "build-your-own" sundaes. Provide vanilla ice cream and toppings such as chocolate and caramel sauce, whipped cream, chocolate sprinkles, sliced bananas, maraschino cherries.

Salad Bar

Here's a nice alternative to serving a hot meal after church, and it's easy to put together. Purchase or have group members bring the ingredients: lettuce, tomatoes, alfalfa sprouts, cheese, black olives, cucumber, carrot, fresh mushrooms, salad dressings, sunflower seeds, croutons, bacon bits. You might also include pickled beets, deviled eggs, pickles, etc. People build their own salads and pay a set price or make a donation.

Continental Breakfast

You might plan this fundraiser in conjunction with a special Sunday in your church, such as the Annual Meeting. Several weeks ahead, meet to plan the menu. You might offer several options. For example,
Fruit cup OR juice (Orange or Apple)
Tea OR coffee
Large muffin OR croissant OR bagel (with cream cheese)
Cheddar cheese

Copy of the morning paper (or Annual Report, or church newsletter, etc.)

Announce the event in church. Set a cost for the breakfast and take orders the week ahead. On the Saturday before, pack individual orders in brown paper bags and label them with names. Have congregation members pick them up after worship.

Lasagna Dinner and Auction

It is probably best to sell tickets to this event so you will know how much food to make. The group might make and freeze lasagnas ahead of time, or ask a dozen or so members of the congregation to donate a lasagna. Serve with a tossed or Caesar salad. Dinner is followed by the auction.

To organize an auction: You will need members of the congregation to donate a talent or item of value to the church. For example, a gourmet meal for four, a boat ride, two tickets to a community theater performance, a "to order" Christmas baked-goods basket for the busy entertainer, use of a cottage for the weekend, a free golf lesson, the loan of a video camera, an offer to rototill a garden. The youth themselves can contribute with nights of free babysitting, or the entire youth group could offer an afternoon of yard cleanup, leaf raking, etc. For this part of the auction you will need an "auctioneer," preferably someone with experience calling bids at an auction (or at least someone with enthusiasm). That makes it entertaining for everyone!

To organize a silent auction: Collect small items such as baked goods, handicrafts, or gift certificates from local businesses to put in a "silent auction." In a silent auction, items are displayed on tables and people place their written bids and names on a sheet of paper corresponding to each item. Then stand back and watch the bidding wars begin! The highest bid wins, and only the highest bidder must pay the amount they bid. The silent auction might be open for bidding before and during dinner, but close the bidding before the real auction begins. Determine what the highest bid is and who the bidder is and reveal the names of these silent auction winners at the end of the auction. Announce where people should pick up their items and pay their bid money.

The Big Blue Box Drive

This is a good fundraiser in the early fall or at spring-cleaning time! Make an announcement several weeks ahead of time to give people time to gather items they would like to recycle or have hauled to the dump. For a fee, offer to pick up items from their home for recycling such as newspapers, plastic, aluminum cans, corrugated or box board, and items for disposal at the dump. Provide a list of items that your local landfill will accept and specify any items you cannot accept (e.g. clothing, refrigerators, propane tanks). Gather a list of addresses and arrange for the use of trucks to transport items to the recycling depot or dump. Plan a collection route and inform church members of the approximate time you will pick up items. On a Saturday morning, meet at the church and provide teams of youth with a list of addresses. Plan to regather at the church for sandwiches and cold drinks afterward.

Hot Dog and Pop Sales at Local Grocery Store

Non-profit groups are often able to request the opportunity to sell hot dogs in front of the busy grocery stores on a Saturday or a Sunday afternoon. Just call the manager and encourage your congregation to shop on that day. The stores usually encourage you to buy your supplies from the store. Contact a local Lions or other service club about renting a barbeque. The profits can be amazing!

Recycled Card Sales

Some planning ahead is required for this fundraiser! Invite congregation members to donate greeting cards they no longer wish to keep – e.g. birthday, Christmas, anniversary, thank-you, etc. (Note: Often humorous cards don't work as the "punch line" is printed on the inside of the card.) Cut the picture side of the card off and glue this to a clean piece of folded cardstock (can be purchased in most stationery stores). Create small packages of assorted cards, grouped by themes, and seal in plastic wrap or fold-over clear plastic sandwich baggies tied with a ribbon. Sell packages for $2–5 each.

Sing It with Flowers

Many people like to give flowers at Christmas. Invite members of the congregation to sign up to have the youth group deliver a poinsettia to someone they care about. If your group is musical, you might add a personal touch by singing *We Wish You a Merry Christmas* when you deliver the flowers. Provide small enclosure cards for people to write a message for the recipient. Buy poinsettias from a nursery at a volume discount price. Call ahead to recipients to ensure they are home when the flowers are delivered.

Index

YOUTH SPIRIT